Minimalist Music

Forthcoming in the series:

Vaporwave by Kirk Walker Graves
Field Recordings by Marc Weidenbaum
Noise Music by Natalie Marlin
Bollywood by Shwetant Kumar
Neo-Soul by Matthew Allen
Pub Rock by Mark Wilkerson
Alterlatino by Javier A. Rodríguez-Camacho
Musique Concrete by Christian Kriticos
Queercore by Audrey Golden
Midwest Emo by Will Hagle

Minimalist Music

George Grella, Jr.

BLOOMSBURY ACADEMIC

NEW YORK · LONDON · OXFORD · NEW DELHI · SYDNEY

BLOOMSBURY ACADEMIC

Bloomsbury Publishing Inc, 1359 Broadway, New York, NY 10018, USA
Bloomsbury Publishing Plc, 50 Bedford Square, London, WC1B 3DP, UK
Bloomsbury Publishing Ireland, 29 Earlsfort Terrace, Dublin 2, D02 AY28, Ireland

BLOOMSBURY, BLOOMSBURY ACADEMIC and the Diana logo are trademarks
of Bloomsbury Publishing Plc

First published in the United States of America 2026

A catalog record for this book is available from the Library of Congress.

ISBN: PB: 979-8-7651-2344-7
           ePDF: 979-8-7651-2346-1
           eBook: 979-8-7651-2345-4

Series: 33 1/3 Genre

Typeset by Integra Software Services Pvt. Ltd.
Printed and bound in the United States of America

For product safety related questions contact productsafety@bloomsbury.com.

To find out more about our authors and books visit www.bloomsbury.com and
sign up for our newsletters.

For all the people I love

Contents

1 What a Word's Worth

"Work from Home with Minimalism,"[1] an eight-hour playlist on the Tidal streaming service with tracks from music by Reich, Glass, Riley, John Adams, Michael Nyman, Arvo Pärt, William Duckworth, and yes Brian Eno, is coming through the speakers as I type this sentence. There's another one next to it on the app's interface titled "Minimalism for the Mind,"[2] which is heavier on Nyman, and has some John Cage and Howard Skempton sprinkled in. In the "More Albums by …" section of the screen, there are other mood-based playlists like "Minimalism: Winter Nights" and "A Minimal Space" that swing more toward Pärt and, interestingly, Morton Feldman. However these are put together, either by a human being or (more likely) through an algorithm, they are delivering music that was once deeply avant-garde art music—and in the case of Feldman still is—to a mass audience.

There was a stir in the circles of people who make and/or listen to new and avant-garde music in 2010 when Martin Scorsese's *Shutter Island* hit movie theaters, because the soundtrack was packed with excerpts from some big names in twentieth-century composition, including Cage, Feldman, Alfred Schnittke, Lou Harrison, the singular microtonal Italian composer Giacinto Scelsi, and Ingram Marshall's incredible ambient chamber piece *Fog Tropes*. There's always the hope

[1]   https://tidal.com/browse/album/136290656?u.
[2]   https://tidal.com/browse/album/143425559?u.

that this kind of exposure will bring new audiences to the music, but while films have presented some of the most avant-garde ideas in modern and contemporary music to mass audiences—the great example being how Stanley Kubrick appropriated Ligeti's startling work for *2001: A Space Odyssey*—there's no evidence that any of them added to that audience of listeners in any appreciable amount.

Perhaps these musical experiences are too tied into the visual medium they support to be interesting enough when separated from the films. As great as Ligeti and Feldman and Scelsi are, there're no service-curated playlists built around their music. And they remain clearly in the avant-garde precincts of classical music, even as Ligeti's Études for piano are in the canon of masterpieces for the instrument. Another way to look at it is that even though these composers' ideas are as old, if not older, than minimalism, they are part of a world of music-making that, for social and capitalist reasons, is a tiny niche in the public consciousness.

The exception is a once avant-garde music known as "minimalism." One of the most famous and often-heard living American composers is Philip Glass, and he was once a hard-core avant-gardist. He never left his avant-garde ways behind, just added things to them and seen them added to the musical world around him, and he's heard on stage, screen, and even in animated sitcoms, and is one of the great opera composers in history. Steve Reich is probably less famous, but the diamond-like brilliance of his ideas has influenced music far and wide, from hip-hop to progressive rock and beyond. One work of his had ramifications for the music business that are still rippling through popular culture. And this all started for him with two tapes loops spinning on two different tape machines in an electronic music studio.

This is a book about how that happened, a book about minimalist music as a genre. That means it's not about musicians like Steve Reich (born 1936) and Philip Glass (born 1937) per se, nor is it a survey of minimalism via lists of composers and their works, or albums, or musicians who play minimalist music. There's plenty of all that, and plenty of Reich and Glass, in the pages to follow. The story concentrates on those two because they have made the most substantial and influential minimalist—and the most *specifically* minimalist—music, and so are the best examples to show the substance and range of minimalism as a genre; what makes it minimalist, how it works, what it means, and why it's important. Their musical careers are literally intertwined at their personal roots and those of minimalism: they were graduate-level classmates at Juilliard, studying under the same composition teachers; from about 1967 through the early '70s, the two composed for and performed with a shared ensemble that only later divided into Steve Reich and Musicians and the Philip Glass Ensemble; they created the music with two different but complementary techniques and sets of influences; and they had a long and acrimonious split over the question of whether or not Reich showed minimalist language to Glass or if the latter developed it on his own. This was only reconciled in September 2014, when the two took the stage at the Brooklyn Academy of Music to, with other musicians, play Reich's *Four Organs*. Beyond personal drama, the story is about how minimalism would not exist without the two. So if none of your favorites are inside, I apologize in advance, and I'm also certain you'll find the pathways that lead to your favorites, and ideas and other music that will have you appreciating your favorites even more.

One reason you may not find your faves is that by necessity this is a short book, but as Igor Stravinsky and other great artists have pointed out, limits are a vital and useful precondition for making any work, they focus the purpose and the means, they set a beginning and an end, borders to fill with ideas. The hard border here is itself the purpose of this book, to argue for just what minimalist music is, which means excluding things it isn't. That's not pejorative on any music not within, it's simply that there's only so much that can fit, and that the definition of minimalism you'll find that follows is different in a crucial way from most others. Minimalism is clearly not the only satisfying genre, but it is one that not only stands out prominently as a specific thing, but is one of the most important genres since the middle of the twentieth century, and as will be explored also has deep and vital historical significance.

Seeing what the genre is, and seeing where it first appeared in history, explains why some of your faves might not be in here. Also, some whom so far pretty much every analysis of minimalism has included are not in here. This is not a provocation, it's setting a border—a definition—and then seeing what fits inside and what doesn't.

First, it's essential to establish an understanding of the word itself, which has always been more than a little fraught. That's standard in music history, people working within a genre that has been defined from the outside (like jazz, which even Miles Davis dismissed as a term) are often uncomfortable, at the least, with its label. Reich and Glass have never liked minimalism as a term. Reich told choreographer Anne Teresa de Keersmaeker, who has made dances that physically illustrate the processes of his music, "As to what I call what I do, I have no name for it other than 'music.'"[3] In his memoir, relating how his early composing was for the theater, Glass relates, "'If you're not a

---

[3] Steve Reich, *Conversations* (Toronto: Hanover Square Press, 2022), 241.

minimalist, what are you?' Many have asked over the course of my career. 'I'm a theater composer,' I reply."[4]

But the reason we have words is so that we can communicate information and meaning, and minimalism is a word we have that communicates a lot of both, and minimalism has long been cemented as the word that automatically refers to Reich, Glass, La Monte Young (born 1935), Terry Riley (born 1935), Meredith Monk (born 1942), and many others who we'll find don't really fit into that term. Nor does everyone in that list. Minimalism is in our language, and if, like so many words, its meaning can be fudged, then this book means to be an extended definition and reference toward clarifying it.

That's easier to do with sixty years of the music behind us; the shape and direction of minimalist music are clear in the accumulated body of work. It's also important to do, because the term and the understanding of it have been somewhat haphazard from the start. Minimalism is an accidental word for this music, one of several key accidents of history, without which the genre would never have been created. Michael Nyman, one of the most prominent minimalist composers around, began using the term "minimal music" in the music criticism he was writing in the late 1960s to label something he heard in certain avant-garde circles. It first appeared in a column he wrote for *The Spectator*, October 11, 1968, and referred to a piece he had heard by Danish composer Henning Christiansen, who was part of the Fluxus movement. It was a spur-of-the-moment way to describe the memory of an aural experience, and at the time had nothing at all to do with Reich, Glass, Terry Riley, et al. But it worked, and it stuck, and it can't be unstuck.

4   Philip Glass, *Music without Words: A Memoir* (New York: Liveright, 2015), 128.

But it is too generic, and it confuses, in the archaic meaning of the word, a manner of making music with a manner of making painting and sculpture which, though they are historically and socially coincident, have nothing to do with each other. Painting and sculpture are objects, music is sound waves, an active physical property that has no permanent existence and that outside of massively reverberant spaces like cathedrals and cisterns has a duration measured in seconds, if that. A Donald Judd sculpture, a monochromatic Frank Stella painting, a Dan Flavin fluorescent light installation all sit or hang in space. You go to see them, look, and move on. Music from Reich or Glass comes to you, it produces sound waves that reach out, touch you, then are replaced by the next wave, etc., until it all stops. It has no other dimensions other than your experience. There is simply no connection between the static materials of the plastic arts and the organized vibrations of sound.

There is, however, an interesting connection between a specific, but uncommon, type of information in the visual arts and music: Sol LeWitt's wall drawings have the same conception as a musical score; they are instructions given to others for them to follow to produce something. A musical score is an instruction set for how to make certain sounds that are organized in time, a LeWitt wall drawing is an instruction set for how to apply a set of shapes and colors on a wall.[5] A composer and LeWitt can participate in this, but never have

---

[5]   His *Wall Drawing #260* (1975) at the Museum of Modern Art has, like all of them, the instructions in the subtitle: "On Black Walls, All Two-Part Combinations of White Arcs from Corners and Sides, and White Straight, Not-Straight, and Broken Lines." https://www.moma.org/collection/works/79898.

to, and both a composer's music and LeWitt's drawings can be made after their deaths—the instructions are preserved and the work is still theirs. Even passed on, they exist in the moment of live reproduction. The wall drawings also take two steps closer to minimalist music in that they are usually impermanent, created for an exhibition then destroyed when the show is over, and both use a limited set of simple ideas that can combine to produce maximal (in physical space or time) results. It is a non-minimalist artist, Chuck Close (who made a famous portrait of Glass), whose work comes much closer to minimalist music in the way he used small cells of abstract images as something like puzzle pieces to create a large-scale, clear representation—this is the way single repeated measures in minimalist music, extended through time, create complete works.

Tom Johnson, an important minimalist composer and an equally important critic who covered the early years of minimalism as it developed at its source in New York City for *The Village Voice*, laid out a popular and very catholic definition in the introduction to the collection of his writings, *The Voice of New Music: New York City 1972–1982*:

#

> The idea of minimalism is much larger than most people realize. It includes, by definition, any music that works with limited or minimal materials: pieces that use only a few notes, pieces that use only a few words of text, or pieces written for very limited instruments, such as antique cymbals, bicycle wheels, or whisky glasses. It includes pieces that sustain one basic electronic rumble for a long time. It includes pieces made exclusively from recordings of rivers and streams. It includes pieces that move in endless circles. It includes pieces that set up an unmoving wall of

saxophone sound. It includes pieces that take a very long time to move gradually from one kind of music to another kind. It includes pieces that permit all possible pitches, as long as they fall between C and D. It includes pieces that slow the tempo down to two or three notes per minute.[6]

#

In the *Voice*, Johnson labeled music by Gavin Bryars, David Tudor (one of John Cage's important collaborators), Phill Niblock, Ingram Marshall, and others as minimalism, and also wrote of Glass's famous, monumental opera *Einstein on the Beach*, "This may be minimalism in a kind of sociohistoric sense, but it has little to do with the purer minimalism of other composers."[7] I disagree with this. Johnson's definition isn't right or wrong, as being about something other than minimalist music. His view is that minimalism is all about the materials, which would be useful for the plastic arts but leaves out the crucial step in music, which is how those materials are organized. He may have been thinking of Annea Lockwood's wonderful *A Sound Map of the Hudson River* when saying minimalist music "includes pieces made exclusively from recordings of rivers and streams," because that work is a set of field recordings of the Hudson from its origin in streams leading out of Henderson Lake in the Adirondacks down to Upper New York Bay. Already, there's an argument over how minimal using a river as material is; even if it is only one thing, surely the mass, variety, and complexity destroys the notion of being minimalist. As a physical object a river is a river, as a sound, a river is seemingly infinite details of motion, timbres, and dynamics. What Johnson seems to be

---

[6] Tom Johnson, *The Voice of New Music: New York City 1972–1982* (Paris: Editions 75, 2002), 5.

[7] Ibid, 259.

defining is his own experiences of music made with certain source materials, and thinking as a plastic artist, rather than a composer. It's poetic and compelling, but not useful for examining genre. It describes impressions, but hardly any compositional ideas and methods.

That is a crucial thing. This book—and Johnson's critical writing—is about what composers have made because minimalism is a composer's music, and that means it is an explicitly classical music. It always has been and the core always will be (though that core is just a starting point, as will be explored). "Classical" is even more fraught in public discussions than "minimal" because it has heavy and damaging extra-musical connotations of class elitism and social snobbery—which it has richly earned! It is also considered "art" music as opposed to "popular" music, which has been an unfortunate way to give art music a bad name. But again, all this is extra-musical, the contents of the music itself, and its history, have been mostly neglected by the institutional marketing of classical music over the past century, and are very different from the modern public perception. Minimalist music began inside that long history and exemplifies the actual history, social presence, and importance of the music in more honest and meaningful ways than any orchestra or opera administrator can seem to grasp.

Minimalist music, as classical music and as art—meaning simply an abstract music constructed primarily by notating ideas on paper and not made with the capitalist music marketplace in mind—music, is a way to see what that history is, what it has always meant socially and musically, and what it still can mean now and in the future. It has also been immensely appealing to general audiences, because abstraction (music that isn't about anything other than how the notes fit together) and art (music that has some sense of idealized self-knowledge and sincerity to it and is free from attempts to pander to notions of what listeners might want) can easily be just as interesting and satisfying as anything by Taylor Swift, Radiohead, or A Tribe Called Quest. There are always a lot more curious and open-minded listeners out there than either commercial record labels or classical music institutions think there are.

To go back to first terms, I also disagree with Nyman. Or better, I disagree with what has generally been taken from what on his part was a casual statement that was never meant to carry, much less explain, an enormous amount of fantastic music and any critical criteria about or ideology of the same. He wrote "minimal," and that is what I disagree with. So here is my first border: this is a book not about minimal music, that is, music with a minimum of materials; this is a book about minimalist music, a specific type of music defined by not what it's made with but how it's made. Minimalist music may have a minimum of materials, but the latter is not any kind of criteria or of any use in general except within each piece of music itself. Minimalism is not an object, but a method. Nyman has written about this often and cogently through the years, and his simple, off-hand word became much more insightful and meaningful. He made the word first, so he gets the last one here, which comes from the "Minimal music, determinacy, and the new tonality" chapter in his book *Experimental Music: Cage and Beyond*, "One single word might sum up what appears, on the surface at least, to be the most significant quality of experimental music: limitlessness."[8]

[8] Michael Nyman, *Experimental Music: Cage and Beyond* (Cambridge: Cambridge University Press, 1999), 139.

2 Time and Western Man

This is a book about time. Any book, any writing about music is about time in one way or another, because music itself is always about time—it outlines and fills a duration. That may not be the purpose of this or that music-making, but just as a building, whatever its function, must exist in the dimensions of height, width, and depth, music must exist in the dimension of time. The process of putting up a building means defining space, inch by inch. Music also defines the dimension of time, but only the duration in which it exits—listening to a three-minute, thirty-second song takes up that amount of time in the listener's life—and music has to have time in which to unfold, to establish its means and ends, to play through the verse, chorus, and bridge, and to repeat anything.

Primers on music, whether introductory books or lessons or YouTube videos, start with what they consider to be the idea that the fundamental features of music are melody, harmony, and rhythm. Excluding philosophical and conceptual arguments, those are absolutely the most important basic qualities, but they rest on the foundation of time. Time is the single essential feature of music. As sophistic as it might seem to point out that music cannot exist without time, it is both true and vital to note. There is music without rhythm (e.g., drones, and more on this to follow), there is music without harmony (chant), there is music without melody (Bach's Prelude No. 1 in C, BWV 846), but there is no music, none whatsoever, without time. The proof is found in the most extreme philosophical and conceptual idea, John Cage's *4'33"*, conceived and composed in 1952. It's a work about how listeners define music, how they decide what is musical and what isn't. And the only material it uses is the duration in the title.

Because all music has time, all music is about time. Just as all building are about spatial dimensions, and for each that's almost always only the necessary foundation for their existence; buildings are about their function, music is about its expressive purpose. Minimalist music, on the other hand, is prominently about time, and the specific pieces that established it as a genre are only about time. Different examples of it may be about other things too, like the drama and narratives of Philip Glass's *Einstein on the Beach*, Meredith Monk's *Atlas*, and Steve Reich's *Different Trains*, but historically those examples came once the genre had been firmly established and there were opportunities to explore where it could lead, they are post-minimalist. Even those are built on the idea of music that doesn't just have duration but works by structuring time in specific ways and by using the passage of time as the main resource.

That is one of the identifying features of minimalist music: it is a signification of time that shows time happening and shows how music works in time and how music shapes and defines time. Minimalism's workings, its process, are right on the surface—this is again at the core of the genre, that experiencing the process in action is not just essential, but often the entire technique and purpose. Reich's *Pendulum Music* (1968) consists of four microphones, each suspended from some height at the end of long chords, set swinging in front of speakers until their momentum runs out and they stop. The music comes from the feedback that appears each time a mic passes close in front of a speaker. The process is the music; the music is only process, the time it takes depends on the weight and speed and arc of the microphones, the time is marked by each mic swing so it can be seen passing as well as heard. It is a music of time.

The simplest things can be the most profound. There's a performance of *Pendulum Music* on Sonic Youth's 1999 album *Goodbye 20th Century* (Sonic Youth Records) that lasts for five minutes, fifty-six seconds of clock time. But the time in the music continually slows down as the swinging microphones lose momentum. If we push this just a little bit further, really just look at the surface, we see that the piece is about more than how it sounds, it's about the relative nature of time. The experience *in* time *of* time is a combination of the physical properties of the universe and the individual, subjective psychology of the feeling of time. Maybe you follow the changing time of the microphones and feel the dimension slowing, maybe you see or hear the microphones and feedback, but time feels steady, maybe the piece is boring and you feel impatient for it to end, which might be a combination of the time *Pendulum Music* is taking to finish feeling endless and something speeding up internally to get it the hell over with.

Time is relative in *Pendulum Music*, and it's relative as a physical property as well, as Einstein (not on a beach) realized and described. And as a work that is about the physics of motion, sound waves, and time, this modest, simple conceptual little thing could be a model of the Big Bang and evolution of the universe to the point of heat death, when time will come to an end. That wasn't Reich's design, he was experimenting with things and seeing where he could push the process of his music. Later Reich pieces, and minimalism generally, have a ticking-clock-like quality that is not just the sound of notes and rhythms coming together, coordinated in time, but the sound of the present turning into the future. That process is deep, it's all around us, it runs through us, it's our lives. Reich wrote about this aspect of minimalism in his important essay "Music as a Gradual Process," something that's not quite a manifesto for a movement but a clear description of what he wanted to hear. He points out that by process, "I do not mean the process of composition, but rather pieces of music that are, literally, processes. The distinctive thing about musical processes is that they determine all the note-to-note (sound-to-sound) details and the over all form simultaneously. (Think of a round or infinite canon.)." Of the listener, he says the experience should be like "pulling back a swing, releasing it, and observing it gradually come to rest; turning over an hour glass and watching the sand slowly run through the bottom; placing your feet in the sand by the ocean's edge and watching, feeling, and listening to the waves gradually bury them."[1]

Simple things can produce transformative experiences—when you're working with time as your medium, and stripping things down so that the construction of time is the mechanics of the music, you reveal profound questions about those experiences. Time is the medium and master of everything, and it is the medium that the processes of minimalist music master, at least for a time. So this is a book about time, about how musicians work with time, about the sensation of hearing time in music, about starting at one point in time and coming out another. It's about the dimension of time in which

[1]   Steve Reich, *Writings on Music* (New York: Oxford University Press, 2002), 34. The essay was first published in the catalog to the Whitney Museum exhibition *Anti-Illusion: Procedures/Materials*, in 1969.

we experience our life and which we have no control over, and about how, culturally and psychologically, the experience of it is not uniform—there's an important dividing line between two different views of what time is for human beings and how it shapes our lives and the directions of societies and civilizations. It's about the perception of music and the perception of time, and how minimalism starts with the mix of the two as its foundation and even raison d'être.

Time is the reason so many minimalist works just end in a way that—to ears and sensibilities trained on music like songs, sonatas, or symphonies that are formed so that they move through harmonies and time to get to a point where the mechanics and emotions resolve, where all settles on a final chord at a final moment, like the period at the end of a book—feels abrupt. Minimalism is not about wrapping a set of lyrics in a song form so that they state and rest their case, like an argument, it's not about a musical sentimental education that starts in a home key (E-flat major, for example) and journeys through many other harmonies and modulations to other keys (say, C minor or A-flat major) before, wiser and more experienced, it returns with a sense of finality and maybe even triumph to E-flat. Changing harmonies and keys may be prominent in minimalist music, especially with Glass and late works from Reich, but even those usually just stop, because the main idea in the music is to work with time, to set out a pulse and keep marking marking marking marking marking marking marking it, like the second hand on a clock, until the music's time has come to an end. All those other musics, again, exist in time and work with it by building a self-contained world within time.

One way to think of it is that most music is similar, in the dimension of time, to movies and television shows. Within a certain duration the visual narrative starts and then proceeds until a narrative end point, at which it stops. That is, the story is complete, and the duration of it is determined by the accumulation of images, dialogue, etc., that make up that story. Most of the music we experience (at least in the West) is the same way, it has some sort of story to tell. Maybe it's a song like "Crazy in Love." The recording closes on a vamp that fades down, but by then the song has ended because its story, in verse and chorus, is done, and that's what the fade-out is saying, "we're all done, see ya." In abstract music, Beethoven's Symphony No. 5 ends on repeated C Major chords because every note that preceded those, from the famous opening da-da-da-dahhh, points to not only the finality of the harmonic resolution of all the tension Beethoven built but to the number of times those chords are heard. Beyoncé's purpose is to tell you she's crazy in love, in song, and Beethoven's purpose is to spin out an abstract emotional drama that ends in satisfaction. Time is the dimension in which those stories unfold.

There's just as much finality in the way Reich's *Drumming* or Philip Glass's *Music in Twelve Parts* ends as "Crazy in Love" or Symphony No. 5, but it's a different kind. It's the finality of the clock hitting 5:00 p.m. after a day at an office job, of the train pulling into its destination right on schedule, even the kitchen timer going off. It is the moment of stillness after a process has stopped, even if it hasn't finished. That's another way to look at it: Beyoncé and Beethoven finish in time, *Drumming* and *Music in Twelve Parts* stop in time. Is there still work to finish at 5:00 p.m. but that can be done the next day? Does the train go on to farther stops? Is the timer marking the next step in cooking? Each is a stopping point but not a conclusion.

The simplest things can be the most profound. The difference between stopping and finishing is a slight thing and also an enormous thing. Music that finishes has something it needs to say and then finish saying, there's a teleology involved. Music that stops—specifically minimalist music—has no inherent teleology. It has workings and processes, and as Reich puts it in an idealized way, " … once the process is set up and loaded it runs by itself."[2] That's not literal, as people, not machines, play his music. But it opens the way to further understanding of just what this process is. "What I'm interested in is a compositional process and a sounding music that are one and the same thing," he writes, "We all listen to the process together since it's quite audible, and one of the reasons it's quite audible is because it's happening extremely gradually," in time. "Even when all the cards are on the table, and everyone hears what is gradually happening in a musical process, there are still enough mysteries to satisfy all." And he acknowledges the subliminal idea in music that has a process that stops without regard to finishing, that it may continue indefinitely in memory and imagination, or some philosophical dimension: "Listening to an extremely gradual musical process opens my ears to *it* [original emphasis], but *it* always extends farther than I can hear … sounds moving out away from intentions, occurring for their own acoustic reasons, is *it*."[3]

He recognized how time was the medium and the means for this process music, clarifying, "By 'gradual' I mean extremely gradual; a process happening so slowly and gradually that listening to it resembles *watching a minute hand on a watch— you can perceive it moving after you stay with it a little while* [emphasis added]."[4] At the time Reich wrote this, he had already

---

2   Ibid, 34.
3   Ibid, 35.
4   Ibid, 36.

made his important tape pieces *It's Gonna Rain* and *Come Out*, and had composed *Piano Phase*, *Violin Phase*, and *Pendulum Music*. He heard these processes and was laying them out in his music. These pieces are about the possibilities of patterns of sound gradually changing through time, the aural equivalent to watching that minute hand.[5]

The listening experience and his words on process move us toward a definition of minimalist music as a genre. Genres are meaningless as marketing categories but have consequence as characteristics for a type of thinking or work. They are limits not in a controlling sense but in how they set boundaries within which an artist can create something, and push new ideas and innovations that expand or subvert those boundaries. Genre limits are like word counts and deadlines for a writer, they focus and organize thoughts, goals, and means. They also set criteria for what works and what doesn't, and what fits and what doesn't.

Reich addressed that as well. He recognized that other music, like "Indian classical and drug-oriented rock and roll may make us aware of minute sound details … rather than on key modulation, counterpoint, and other peculiarly Western devices. Nevertheless, these … musics … are not processes. The distinctive thing about musical processes is that they

---

[5]   The tape pieces come from field recordings of speech, the first of street preacher Brother Walter in Union Square, San Francisco, the second the voice of Daniel Hamm, a young Black man who was part of the Harlem Six, a prominent civil rights case and criminal trial in the mid-1960s—Reich was asked to make an audio collage of taped interviews as a benefit for the defendants, and used a short segment separately to make *Come Out*. There is text inside those two that is complex, fascinating, and important ground for social and political analysis, but for now the sound and how it exemplifies Reich's thoughts about process is the key.

determine all the note-to-note details and the overall form simultaneously."[6] This is the key statement; a hint of not just what minimalist music in Reich's view might sound and feel like, not what it does, but how it's made that way. If the goal is the experience of gradual moment-to-moment change that, after a longer duration, is perceived as an enormous change, what are the means?

#

Music is repetition and change, within each piece and in the overall course of music. Having only time with which to work, music lays out sequences of organized sonic events through linear time. It has no physical properties—other than reaching and literally touching the listener via sound waves—or dimensions. Musical analysis often uses terms like "structure" and "form" to describe identifiable abstract features like counterpoint or a C Major chord (structures) or say this thing is a song, that is a sonata-allegro movement (forms). These can be preserved on recordings or written down, where they can be heard or read in music notation, but they do not exist. Except in time, which means that for us to hear these things come into shape through time, to hear that the chorus has arrived in a song, or that the first eight-bars of a Haydn symphony have passed, and to enjoy the uncanny and wonderful pleasure of anticipating their return, this sequences of sounds have to be apprehensible to our listening and stick in the memory long enough that there is a certain order that makes sense and is satisfying.

Nearly every bit of music in existence uses repetition and change. Here's one: "Do-Re-Mi"[7] from Rodgers and

---

[6]   Reich, *Writings on Music*, 36.
[7]   Published by the Hal Leonard Corporation.

Hammerstein's musical *The Sound of Music*. The melody that carries each full verse is built through a series of repetitions and changes to what's being repeated:

1. "Doe, a dear, a female dear" uses three repeated notes.

2. "Ray, a drop of golden sun" repeats with the material from 1 then extends and raises it in pitch.

3. "Me, a name I call myself" is 1 just higher in pitch.

"That will bring us back to Do, oh oh oh"; small, repeated units, gradual changes to them, complete the cycle of the song, which then returns to the beginning and is performed as a canon, a structure grounded in repetition. It's simple and it shows how repetition works in music, by establishing an idea in the listener and then setting out contrasts to that.

As musicologist Elizabeth Hellmuth Margulis writes, "Music unfolds dynamically, note by note … a performance cannot be taken in all at once; listeners must orient to each passing musical moment using memory systems to reconstruct events that have passed, perceptual systems to take in events that are presently sounding, and predictive mechanisms to anticipate what might happen next."[8] This is the description of a process and how it works, "dynamically" through time, "note by note," listeners perceiving events and how they relate to previous events, through time. Recall that Reich wrote, "The distinctive thing about musical processes is that they determine all the note-to-note details and the overall form simultaneously."

It is obvious that one of the main, and the most immediate, characteristics of minimalist music is that it uses repetition.

---

[8]   Elizabeth Hellmuth Margulis, *The Psychology of Music: A Very Short Introduction* (New York: Oxford University Press, 2019), 49.

But then so does almost all but the most experimental or conceptual stuff. Even drone and noise music build structures and forms along linear time. And those structures and forms only become apparent through how the drone or noise changes; even these seemingly abstract and monolithic sounds can and ideally do change, the drone of a steady held note can shift in timbre through time, noise can be washed with filters so its quality transforms. Neither may have any repetition—they're often just sustained—but the intentional shaping of even steady sounds like these, through time, is a significant way to organize them as music, and why the background hum of current and electronic devices is part of our soundscape, but isn't music in the critical sense.

Instead it is the note-to-note details, the getting from one note to the next and one moment in time to the next, that make minimalist music. Those notes form repeating patterns, impress themselves into memory. The note-to-note movement and repetition continues, but gradually shifts; e.g., a four-note pattern repeats four times, then it becomes five notes, and that repeats four times, then six notes, etc. Notes get added to the end, and taken from the beginning, and eventually it's a four-note pattern as at the start, but a completely *different* one. The minute hand moves. The music repeats and by repeating changes. It shows the progression of time in its sound and its bones, because that's all it means to do. Minimalist music is process music that marks the passage of time as both its foundational method and its sound. The distinction that it marks time in a way that's at least a metaphor for a watch is essential; minimalist music has duration not to fill time but to show time passing. This is another reason why one of its features is that it stops rather than finishing. Minimalism processes time, and is the process of time put into organized sound.

Physicist Richard A. Muller argues in his book *Now: The Physics of Time* that time is a property of space, and that the reason we have time that predictably keeps moving into the future—which is both how it is you can keep moving on to the next word in this book after you finish reading this one and how music can even exist, much less define a temporary abstract structure that connects past to present—is because the universe keeps expanding. That is, as the universe keeps moving outward from the central point of the Big Bang, it creates new space in which to expand, and that time is a property of space. Each new bit of space created means one additional moment of time.

But there is time as a property of the universe, and there is time as human experience, a dimension in which to think and write and make music. There is history as a product of time, the memory and record of what has gone before. With that understanding, there can be no deeper, more insightful, elegant, or meaningful depiction of the physical nature of time in music—and nothing describes time better than music does—than minimalism.

As a genre, minimalism is not defined by style. Of course, there are significant examples of the how it can be realized as a style, but those are matters of taste for the musicians who make the music. The two most important minimalist composers, Reich and Glass, have extraordinarily different styles, and are both absolutely minimalists, they more than any others define the genre. It's also significant that Reich and Glass are composers in the classical tradition, because minimalism is classical music at its roots, and what that means in terms of music history and culture will be essential to examine. But genre-wise, it is a practice, and so it can fit into nearly any style of music, and how it has done is part of the story of minimalism in musical (and non-musical) culture.

But it can't fit into every style of music. And here is where the standard story of minimalism needs rev sion. The conventional definition of minimalism leads to ccrralling a group of composers and musicians that is so broad, with so many who simply don't share the practice of minimalism, that it's worthless. It's no judgment on the quality and importance of the music of any of these artist to point out that Steve Reich's work has nothing to do with Brian Eno's, which has nothing to do with Annie Gosfield's, which has nothing to do with John Luther Adams's, which has noth ng to do with Max Richter's, et al., etc., ad nauseam. Pop song arrangements that use *minimal* instrumental material but don't use *minimalist* processes, like Lorde's "Royals," don't fit in. Minimalist music can be maximal in duration and also musical activity, because the process doesn't prescribe either, but *minimal* music by definition can't be maximal (except in duration). Nor can ambient music be part of the story, because it works with time in a way that is the opposite of minimalist processes.

Another music that, because of how it works with time, can't be minimalist is drone music. That it has been thought of as minimalist for decades is in part the confusion of minimalist with minimal, and also because of the received wisdom about the origins of the genre. Histories of the music, including fine ones from Wim Mertens, Michael Nyman, Keith Potter, K. Robert Schwarz, and Edward Strickland, and critical writing from Kyle Gann, Tom Johnson, and others, state that the founders are La Monte Young, Terry Riley, Reich, and Glass. Young was indeed there at the proto-stage of minimalism. His connection with Riley alone makes him an important figure, and the sheer quality and influence of his music speak for themselves. Like the minimalists, he makes music in a way that is a practice, not a style, so it has reached far and deep through the decades. He has been the metaphorical father of music that has brought together the Western classical avant-garde, non-Western spiritual and aesthetic traditions, avant-garde rock and proto-punk, and the unclassifiable, free-floating world of drones, minimal music, and improvisation. As a teen jazz musician in Los Angeles, Young crossed paths with Don Cherry and Eric Dolphy. He was a collaborator with or inspiration to many of the key artists across multiple media in the 1960s. His "time and harmonic influence on the methodology and terminology of Andy Warhol, the Velvet Underground (via John Cale), Terry Riley, Tony Conrad, Charlotte Moorman, Cornelius Cardew, Henry Flynt, Nam June Paik, Dick Higgins, Rhys Chatham, and Brian Eno, among others, proves the point."[9]

His legacy is like an immense tree growing equally far in both branches and roots. Immense, but the music is drones or improvisatory explorations of tuning systems, not minimalist. That he is consequential is indisputable, but La Monte Young is not part of the definition of minimalist music. But he is part of the story.

#

Culture does not appear and develop in a vacuum, with the exception of one single, necessary moment. In his 1947 essay "The First Man Was an Artist," painter Barnett Newman wrote, "Man's first expression, like his first dream, was an aesthetic one. Speech was a poetic outcry rather than a demand for

---

[9] Joseph Nechvatal, "Flawed Composition," *The Brooklyn Rail*, March, 2012. https://brooklynrail.org/2012/03/books/flawed-composition/.

communication."[10] Man evolved into an aesthetic being, created the first stories and images and music, and culture was born. We are the results of the first *Homo aestheticus*, and even the most avant-garde and experimental artists arrive with that ancient lineage within them.

La Monte Young composed his *Trio for Strings* in 1958, when he was in graduate studies with Seymour Shifrin at the University of California, in Berkeley, and this is where he and Terry Riley met. The *Trio for Strings* is written for a quartet of violin, viola, and two cellos but has only three instrumental lines, the title has to do with the notes that are heard rather than the ensemble. This is drone music, or something so close to it that no other description makes much sense; long sustained pitches interrupted by long stretches of quiet. There is very little musical material. Being a drone, rhythm is irrelevant and nonexistent, there aren't a lot of notes within each sustained duration, which is either minimal or not, depending on the point of view. The lack of rhythm is exceedingly important for how to see what the music is; repetition and rhythm are inseparable, a composer needs rhythms in order to make anything repeat. In the most sophistic sense, there is repetition in *Trio for Strings* because after first playing, then pausing, the musicians play again. But they are repeating an action, they are not playing music that uses identifiable repetition to process itself from one place in time to another or even to create a feeling that time is being marked into regular segments.

For the piece, Young took the twelve notes of the chromatic scale and slowly layered them, three at a time. He was originally

---

[10]   Barnett Newman, *Barnett Newman: Selected Writings and Interviews*, ed. John Philip O'Neill (Berkeley: University of California Press, 1992), 158.

working through serialism, the dominant compositional ideology in America at the time, and using that in an entirely radical way—drones weren't a thing that high-modernist classical composers did.

But Young was not just thinking about classical music but jazz and Indian music and Japanese music. *Trio for Strings* is a doorway into the mind of a young artist rethinking their path and purpose, and itself has become something that Young has rethought in significant ways. For one, he moved the notes away from the chromatic scale and toward the just intonation tuning system. The original version was long enough that Shifrin was adamant it wouldn't work and Young's peers found it baffling, while the more recent version, as heard on the one recording (*La Monte Young: Trio for Strings*, Dia Art Foundation, 2021) that's been made, takes about three hours across four LPs.

The music is static, which was the original goal, one that has grown more concerted through the decades. At the performance recorded for the album, listeners took off their shoes, lounged or lay down on the carpet, and were not only silent and still for the performance but were asked to leave quietly at the end, with no applause. This wasn't music about watching the minute hand on a watch, or feeling the sand slowly cover your feet, it was about having an experience outside of time, a temporary still point in the life of the universe created by the music.

Even though he treats him as a founder of minimalism, Strickland does have doubts about Young belonging to the genre. But his questions are about tonality and space. *Trio for Strings'* original atonality goes against the notion that minimalist music must be tonal, and if it all flows from Young it clearly does not. The long pauses also work against the continual, gradual development and change in minimalism.[11]

The drone divides Young from minimalist music. But he had opened a door that Riley stepped through. Riley told K. Robert Schwarz:

#

> The main feature in La Monte's music in those days was the total disruption of time as I knew it. It was like being in a time capsule and floating out in space somewhere and waiting for the next event to happen … it was probably my first introduction to a Zen-like approach to the present, not waiting for the next thing to come along, but simply enjoying what's happening right then.[12]

#

That sensibility of "simply enjoying what's happening right then" is a nice fit for what Young was doing with drones and what Riley would do, for a short time, with minimalism. In a graduate-level composition program at a leading university in the San Francisco Bay Area in the middle of the twentieth century, it was countercultural. Context matters, though, and even though this was new for 1958, at least in America, at the foundation there was something ancient, even in the West.

The experience of minimalist music is, on top of whatever happens inside the listener's mind and body, the flow of external time, hearing the music move steadily into

---

[11] Edward Strickland, *Minimalism: Origins* (Bloomington and Indianapolis: Indiana University Press, 2000), 123.

[12] K. Robert Schwarz, *Minimalists* (London: Phaidon Press, 1996), 28.

the future. The experience of *Trio for Strings* is to be outside the flow of time and inside a still and contemplative state. That was also the experience of plainchant and organum in the medieval era, music that was an important part of Young's thinking. Plainchant is sung Christian liturgy and dates back to the beginnings of the Church. Plainchant is monophonic, one musical line everyone sings in unison. Toward the end of the first millennia CE, apparently sometime in the late ninth century, at least one more line was added, creating harmony via polyphony, many voices. The style of the music and its contemplative purpose make it drone music, which is found around the world, has been around thousands of years, but that classical music thought it had left behind, if not during the Renaissance then certainly after the Second World War.

This is the context that made Young a radical, and made minimalist music from Riley's *In C* (1964) on just as radical. Both Young and the minimalists were looking for an escape from the compositional technique of serialism, which in the academies after the Second World War was essentially the only practice excepted as valid and serious. That context was a historical paradox, out of the ordinary in the long view of history. When minimalism came along, it seemed like the new thing, and of course it was, but it an odd yet deeply meaningful way it was a restoration of a long traditional process that had been abandoned.

In the medieval era, there was no such thing as classical music. When Bach was writing fugues, there was no such thing as classical music. When Mozart was composing operas, there was still no classical music. But when Beethoven died in 1827, all of a sudden there was classical music. His impact on the listening public was so great that it essentially established the idea of a past in music, older things that people wanted to preserve and bring back again and again.

Before Beethoven, the music we now call classical that was written by composers on paper for other musicians to play was always new, and made to please the aristocracy, to celebrate important religious and political occasions, and to entertain the public in theaters. As the technology to print music advanced, music was also written for home markets, the way Mozart published his Piano Sonatas to sell to people playing the instrument in their private music rooms.

Since there was no classical music, there was no dividing line between what was supposed to be "art," or "high" music and what was supposed to be "popular." Music meant for different purposes and audiences mixed together. A French song from the Late Middle Ages, "L'homme armé,"[13] was so popular that composers used the tune for dozens of sung masses for choirs. There are surviving examples from Josquin, Palestrina, and du Fay, some of the greatest musicians of the Renaissance. Minuets and marches exist in classical music because composers liked to dance and they saw march music being used to coordinate soldiers in time and space. And what we might now call popular music was borrowing ideas and tunes from classical music. This is just how human culture makes music, always has, always will, a continuous positive feedback loop of things mixing and cooking together.

From the plainchant era up through Beethoven, music in the West also accumulated ideas in a linear progression that

---

[13] The lyrics are about a knight: "The armed man should be feared. / Everywhere it has been proclaimed / That each man shall arm himself / With a coat of iron mail. / The armed man should be feared."

followed the same process happening in science. Monophony developed into polyphony, instrument technology and playing techniques improved. Composers codified more and more details of the symbolic language of music notation. The modern piano brought general agreement on the equal temperament tuning system, with equal frequency distances between notes. All these led to changes in ideas about structure, form, and especially harmony. From monophony to polyphony centered on a central note (modal music) to the more vertical harmonies of chords in the baroque and classical eras, new possibilities of key changes and modulations with equal temperament, ideas about how music could be made almost literally grew both vertically and horizontally.

There were also profound changes in how cultures thought about time. For tens of thousands of years, human beings knew time through the cycles of the seasons, the sun's place in the sky, and through the moon's phases, and during the day appointed times for prayer. For thousands of years, there were sundials and water clocks, then sandglasses. With variations, this is how humans followed time across the globe, and it was a cyclical experience.

That was just as true in medieval Europe as in the rest of the world, and that's where the first clock technology was developed in the thirteenth century so that people knew the proper times for prayer and plainchant. Europe, and the West, became a timekeeping culture, and time was no longer marked by cycles in the days and months and years, but by minutes and hours on the clock,[14] which now seemed to be

[14] Pendulum clocks led to the creation of the metronome for keeping tempos while playing music, the first recognizable modern ones were built in the early nineteenth century. Reich's *Pendulum Music* is made with that very swaying motion, and

accumulating on a linear plot at the same rate and in the same amount no matter how long the sun stayed in the sky. Each moment of the day was being mechanically tracked and marked, and the days now seemed made of hundreds of these markings.

Time and harmony accumulated to the point of instability, with transportation and electrical power-generating technology expressing acceleration and velocity, a subjective rushing sensation, and stacked notes in classical music heading toward an instability that was frighteningly paralleled by a European society that plunged into the madness of the First World War little more than a year after Stravinsky's *Rite of Spring* set an extreme limit to composition. Arnold Schoenberg felt he had found a way past this crisis with a system of atonal composing that, after the upheavals and destruction of the Second World War, looked to composers in Europe and America like a utopia, free of dangerous nationalism and totalitarianism. This came to be called serialism.

Musical terms usually mean more than merely their definitions; they have come to be through long developments in history, and have components that themselves need some understanding so the term itself will be meaningful. "Serial music" and "serialism" are salient examples, because serialism needs some understanding in order to define minimalism (almost everything in music relates to almost every other thing in music, and to music history, and discussing a genre means

György Ligeti's conceptual and sassy *Poème Symphonique* is for 100 metronomes, wound up and allowed to run down at their own pace. That piece is harder and harder to perform as electronic metronomes have become the norm and have mostly replaced mechanical ones.

that idea is going to show itself repeatedly), as the latter came to be in large part as an escape from serialism.

Serialism is a compositional method developed out of Schoenberg's twelve-tone technique, which also needs a definition. Schoenberg's most succinct description of this is a "[m]ethod of composing with twelve tones which are related only with one another."[15] The tones, also known as pitches or notes, make up the entirety of an octave in the common equal-tempered scale in Western music. Starting from A, the standard tuning pitch that orchestras will use before they begin playing, those twelve notes are: A-A#-B-C-C#-D-D#-E-F-F#-G-G#.

Schoenberg devised this technique out of what was a general crisis of tonality in Western classical music that overlapped the turn of the twentieth century. Less a technocrat than a romantic, Schoenberg loved the expressive music of the likes of Johannes Brahms and Gustav Mahler, and heard how the bedrock consonant harmonies, the major and minor keys and chords[16] in which composers wrote and

[15] Arnold Schoenberg, *Composition with Twelve Tones: Chapter 5*, Arnold Schoenberg Center, https://eas.schoenbergmusic.com/composition-with-twelve-tones/schoenberg-12-tone-lecture/chapter-5/.

[16] There are frequency relationships between pitches that have strong and stable, and weak and unstable, qualities, and these come out of the natural overtones (sympathetic, higher frequencies). The first overtone from any given tonic pitch is an octave above, the second is the dominant fifth above that. The overtones extend far, but their physical properties mean that the most stable harmony is the octave, e.g., an A played with the next A above it, while the next most stable is the fifth, e.g., A-E. But the fifth has enough instability and thus tension in it that playing the E alone after an A sets up the need to resolve to A, and the A-E together firmly establishes the general key of A. Whether that's major or minor depends on the third, which is either C# (major) or C (minor). Each would make a triad, and through

on which their music had come to settle at the end of a piece, were disintegrating. He heard this in his own music, which was expressive and, in the case of his famous *Verklärte Nacht* (*Transfigured Night*) for string sextet, hyper-romantic and often emotionally untethered.

What those bedrock harmonies made possible were compositional structures and forms, like counterpoint, fugue, and sonata-allegro, which used tonal relationships along with time for their construction. The disintegration of tonality into atonality, music without a clear central key to which to resolve, threatened the functionality of these forms, which have tremendous use. Schoenberg felt there was no stopping this, but by systematizing it he could keep the old structures and forms relevant. The twelve-tone technique is a set of rules with which to make a scale that uses all the notes in the octave but orders them so that they never define a central key. The central key might disintegrate, but atonal music avoiced that danger. When you build a scale and start using it, you must set out all twelve notes in order before you can start again at the beginning. But you can also use basic compositional techniques of retrograde, inversion, and retrograde-inversion. For example, this twelve-tone scale that Anton Webern used in his Piano Variations, Op. 27 (1936):

\#

B-G-F#-A#-A-G#-D-C-D#-C#-F-E

\#

history the major triad was always felt to be the most stable, while the minor triad was eventually accepted as stable enough to conclude a piece in a darker mood. There are an incredible number of nuances in these relationships to be sure.

In retrograde is:

\#

E-F-C#-D#-C-D-G#-A-A#-F#-G-B

\#

Inverted (upside down):

\#

C-E-F-C#-D-D#-A-B-G#-A#-F#-G

\#

And finally, retrograde-inversion:

\#

G-F#-A#-G#-B-A-D#-D-C#-F-E-C

\#

You can make chords with the notes in any of these scales, as long as you still work through the strict order of the scale, meaning that you can use the inverted row (twelve-tone row is the common term for these scales) and make a chord that is C-E-F, and after that the very next note must be C#.

Regardless of how this sounds to the ear, this works as a compositional system. It is also a pre-compositional procedure, i.e., when a composer decides to write a twelve-tone piece, they first have to go through the procedure of creating a twelve-tone row that follows all the rules. Schoenberg's first full twelve-tone composition was the "Präludium" (1921) section of his Piano Suite, Op. 25 (1921–3). He had been working his way toward this in a free, or essentially un-ruled, atonality, but that was his first public use of his system.

This was not yet serialism, but serialism starts with this. It is more encompassing than twelve-tone, so definitions can't be quite as precise, but it's a way of furthering twelve-tone rules so that they apply to every element in a musical composition. For example, rhythmic serialism would predetermine a twelve-note pattern of rhythms that, like the scale, the composer would have to write through from beginning to end before repeating. Predetermined processes can also apply to dynamics, and just where in the register (e.g., high or low) each pitch will be placed. There are myriad ways to tackle the serialization of the non-pitched features of music, but the underlying concept is to both set out a strict set of rules ahead of time that order, and essentially determine, the musical results, and to integrate all the elements of a piece of music into one concept. And while serialism may be a specifically twentieth-century Western classical music technique, the concept of the details of a piece of music fitting into a syncretic philosophy is not uncommon and is shared by things like Ornette Coleman's harmolodics and Indian classical music.

For a mix of reasons that had to do with a general reaction against the devastation of the Second World War and the possibilities of rebuilding parts of the world out of the rubble, and the increasing movement of classical music away from the public and into universities and specialized institutions, serialism in practice became the method a composer needed to be using in order to succeed in graduate school, and a composer had to succeed in graduate school if they were going to earn a living. This was an acute problem in America, as Strickland points out:

#

The Minimalist Music of Young and others arose during the hegemony of serialism, in which they had been trained and were assumed, as "serious" rather than "popular" composers, to continue … complexity had achieved the status of a professional credential; Serialism, particularly in its American academic institutionalization of received European wisdom, in practice often prized opacity for its own sake as evidence of the ingenuity and sophistication of its composer. Difficulty established one as a "classical" musician in the virtually absolute division between high and low art then prevailing.[17]

Worse than having to make something difficult in order to show one's sophistication—and yet it's harder to write a good song than it is a sonata—is that once you serialize everything, and develop the art of composition into a procedure of predetermining every detail, there's nowhere further for music to go. Utopia turns into something like a Shaker community, prohibiting reproduction and ensuring its own doom. The early minimalists did not want to be part of this cohort, nor were they interested in the opposite pole of aleatoric (chance) music.

The era after the Second World War was the heyday for processes in Western music. The counterexample to serialism was John Cage. Cage is one of the most widely known and, still, least understood radical artists in human history. His name, depending on who hears it, is usually synonymous with one thing; the prepared piano, aleatoric music, his *4'33"* conceptual work. In Cage's music and philosophies, though, these are three different things from three different stretches of his career. Yes, he invented the prepared piano as a way to get more, and unexpected, colors and percussive sounds out of the instrument, but his *Sonatas and Interludes for Prepared Piano* is a fairly conventional new music composition, and one that is based on predetermined rhythmic structures he was using in the 1940s.[18] He also wrote music that was romantic

17   Strickland, *Minimalism: Origins*, 120.
18   Cage was, famously, a student of Schoenberg's at USC in the mid-1930s.

in the sense that he was trying to communicate emotional states to the listener, so that they would feel what it was he had felt—a ubiquitous goal for musicians. But he was ultimately deeply frustrated by this, and a performance of his *Four Walls* for piano and voice left him feeling that it was futile to try and communicate human experience through music.

In 1951, his friend and fellow composer Christian Wolff gave him a copy of the *I Ching*, and Cage started to use it to answer his compositional questions. For example, he could throw the coins and consult the tables in the book to determine what note he should write down. This was the beginning of Cage's monumental and profound chance period. While it took long, hard work and endurance to refine, Cage realized that he could remove any and all conscious and underlying intentions in composition; the kind of thing where a composer might decide on a note or chord because of how they feel to them, he wanted to be rid of that. So for each new work, like *Music of Changes*, he created a pre-compositional process that would determine each musical element based on a chance procedure. This was exceptionally arduous, but also a fruition of his genius, bespoke systems that fit his philosophical and aesthetic values perfectly. And while the results could, to many ears, sound inseparable from those of composers like Milton Babbitt and Pierre Boulez who were using total serialism—if not even more chaotic and incomprehensible—the two sides were deeply at odds on intellectual terms. The suspicion was that Cage, a complete maverick from any other contemporary artistic tradition, was somehow making music that had an impersonality to it that was vital to him, but that sounded like complete serial music through which other composers were trying to say things—something was wrong somewhere. None of them were like Cage, who in his 1949 "Lecture on

Nothing" said: "I have nothing to say / and I am saying it / and that is poetry / as I need it," yet only specialized ears could tell them apart. And that was an important failure of creating music meant for only those ears, a guild making music for a cloistered audience.

But the serialists were certain they were right. Time had brought music to the end of history and an ideal state. That was a product of the illusion and ideology that human progress is as inevitable as the next tick on the clock, as if time will not only heal all our wounds but make us better people, without any responsibility on our part. The Western cargo cult of technology, especially in the last 100 years of radio and audio recordings, films and television, atomic and hydrogen bombs, spaceflight, digital computers and the internet, synthesizers, creates this fantasy. It can make it difficult to see the actual directions of history, and where they culminate. What had seemed from the inside to be the final destination of the steady accumulation of musical knowledge and technique instead turned out to be a cul de sac.

This is not to say that serialism is bad, because it is just one of many tools with which to make music. Any method can be used well or badly, the quality of the music is what matters. The problem is when the tool becomes ideology, and combined with professional structures and the money that flows through them, that ideology becomes the determinant of what matters and what doesn't, what's valid and what isn't. Richard Taruskin wrote in the *Music in the Late Twentieth Century* volume of his *Oxford History of Music*, "During the 1950s and 1960s nearly everyone experimented with [atonal] methods, partly out of curiosity, partly in response to the constant pressure to keep stylistically abreast as mandated by the historicist ideology to which practically everyone, regardless of stylistic orientation or one's artistic convictions, tacitly assented at the middle of the twentieth century."[19] He goes on to note the conformist pressures when a style is dictated by an elite group, e.g., composition professors at Yale, Princeton, and Juilliard, concert programmers at places like Lincoln Center and the major American symphonies and opera companies.

Cage was too singular to be a way out. He is also frequently included in minimalism, because of quiet, delicate, repetitive music like *In a Landscape*. It is lovely but not representative of his whole career, and the intentional process of showing music putting itself together in front of the listener was antithetical to his values.[20] This was the world, then, the world of procedures and predetermination, that Young first began to pry himself from, followed by Riley, and then by Reich and Glass.

#

Minimalism was created specifically as an alternative to both aleatory and serialism and a way to escape that dead end of the latter. All its composers studied music seriously and on a graduate level. One commonality among them that may have pointed them in independent directions is they all had backgrounds around popular music. Young and Riley were terrific jazz players (Riley is a virtuosic keyboardist). Reich studied jazz drumming, played in bands and idolized the great drummer Kenny Clarke, Glass's father owned a record store in Baltimore where Glass worked and listened to music when he

---

[19] Richard Taruskin, *Oxford History of Music: Music in the Late Twentieth Century* (New York: Oxford University Press, 2010), 103.
[20] Reich and Russell Hartenberger, one of his long-time musicians, talked about how Cage came to an open rehearsal for *Music for 18 Musicians*, and afterward went up to Reich and said, "It changed." To this day neither of them knows what he meant. Steve Reich, *Conversations* (Toronto: Hanover Square, 2022), 130.

was a kid—Glass was a big rock fan. All of them were born in the mid-1930s and grew up in an America with radio, movies, LPs, and television. They knew that cultural experiences were repeatable through those mediums.

They also, perhaps, had a better understanding of the meaning and use of classical music history than their colleagues in the academy. The problem with trying to halt music history is that history itself doesn't halt, and one of the greatest things about classical music is that the past is never dead, it isn't even past. Contemporary composers were always learning from music that came before them and using it as the shoulders to stand on so that they might see far; Bach picked up things from Vivaldi, Mozart picked up things from one of Bach's sons, Beethoven learned from Haydn, Brahms learned from Robert and Clara Schumann, Bruckner wrote his own versions of Wagner, Stravinsky moved on from romanticism and created the new style of Neo-classicism by making new music out of things from the past.

Reich, like Young, looked to medieval music, especially twelfth–thirteenth-century French composer Pérotin (and also to Bach and Stravinsky, and Charlie Parker). Both looked to Pérotin's technique of augmentation, elongating a chant melody into a drone then further into a harmony, but they went in wildly different directions. Young transports it, spirituality and all, into modern times as a statement, musical rhetoric. Reich reverse-engineers the technique into process music about altering the original material with time; i.e., minimalism. The opposite of *Trio for Strings* is Reich's *Four Organs*, which he described in conversation with post-minimalist composer Michael Gordon as "totally about augmentation." It's one musical element, a chord (minimal), run through one idea (minimal), to make one of the most exacting and severe minimalist works.

"A chord played for one eighth note gradually becomes 256 beats of held tones with slowly staggered released notes," in other words what he elongates is the marking out of time, the number of beats gradually increasing until they reach their final number. "That would never have happened," he says, "if I hadn't had Pérotin in my head as a kind of basic model. [*Four Organs* is] also the longest [dominant to tonic] cadence in Western music."[21]

Glass has a style that's so different from Reich's that rather than setting them at odds—though they have had personal conflicts between them in their lives—it shows the broad range of possibilities with minimalist technique, and also models the enormous breadth of styles and voices within the important past classical eras (Bach and Georg Friedrich Handel and Jean-Philippe Rameau during the baroque; the founding class cal-era composers Franz Joseph Haydn, Mozart, and Beethoven; Hector Berlioz, Richard Wagner, and Johannes Brahms in the romantic era). Glass is in the long tradition of composers who tell you about themselves through their music. In his memoir, Glass expresses his love for Felix Mendelssohn and Anton Bruckner, and there's a foundation of Mozart and Franz Schubert in the way he uses the traditional virtues of harmony and voice leading. Glass considering himself a theater composer is a shorthand way of explaining that he wants to express narratives through music, whether text-based dramas or the emotional journey of romanticism. As an opera composer, with the except on of *Einstein on the Beach*, his style is an extension of what Mozart and Giuseppi Verdi did in the eighteenth and nineteenth centuries—and even *Einstein* is expressive in this way, just that its subject matter lies outside of standard narratives.

21 Reich, *Conversations*, 62–3.

Glass has also composed many dozen film scores. Like minimalism, that term has come to mean so many different things that it can be confusing. Before movies began to compile various pop songs for their scores in the post-MTV era, classical composers wrote original orchestral music for films. A handful of composers who fled Germany before the Second World War, like Max Steiner and Erich Wolfgang Korngold, became the founding masters of this specialized classical composing, followed by Bernard Herrmann, Ennio Morricone, Toru Takemitsu, Georges Delerue, John Williams, and others, including Glass. Like those names, Glass writes classical music in his modern voice for movie directors. What movies are to modern times, opera was to the nineteenth century, and theater, opera, and film scores are just different and connected facets of the same classical core.[22] And as we'll see, the movies are responsible for Glass becoming a minimalist composer.

Reich, on the other hand, makes music that projects an extroverted, welcoming excitement, but never tries to get the listener to feel anything in particular (with the exception of his own narrative vocal works—words always have meaning). As Glass expresses by design, in the nineteenth-century way, Reich, as he told Micheal Nyman, wants "a blend of controlled individual choice and impersonality," feeling that choosing the material and process was enough and leaving the rest in the hands of the listener.[23] This is also part of a tradition that is in the music Reich loves, like Bach and Stravinsky (but nothing

[22] The reason that early silent films are full of acting with incredibly exaggerated expressions is that many opera singers starred in those movies because they were professionals at expression through gestures, not just voice.

[23] Steve Reich, *Writings on Music* (New York: Oxford University Press, 2002), 92.

from the romantic or even classical eras), who famously (or notoriously) said, "music is, by its very nature, essentially powerless to express anything at all."[24] Reich's instrumental music is as clear as glass as to what he values in how to construct a composition, his sound matches the ideas in "Music as a Gradual Process," but this doesn't open up any windows into his personality. Even his pieces with text, like *Different Trains*, *The Cave*, and *Daniel Variations* show the listener he is thinking about Judaism[25] but keep his inner feelings at a distance.

Music from deep in the history of the classical tradition was always part of Reich and Glass when they began minimalism, even if in their early, experimental years it wasn't always easy to hear. Those years for each, which came to a culmination for both in the first few years of the 1970s, were the experimental ones, the times to try out things and see what worked and didn't to figure out where they wanted to go. When they found that, they dug into the past with greater confidence and clarity and pulled out exactly what it was that was old and that they loved and that they wanted to make new again.

The cycle of the present taking ideas from the past to move everything into the future is how things are done. Minimalism is then not only about how music works with time, but how musical history exists and propagates through time. There are parallel layers here. Repetition in music is a kind of cycle (or loop) that is used to process linear time (like a timeline on a

---

[24]   Igor Stravinsky, *An Autobiography* (New York: Simon and Schuster, 1936), 83.

[25]   One common feature across the first generation (in terms of birth) of minimalist composers is they are all deeply religious, from Riley's shamanism to Reich's Judaism, Glass's Tibetan Buddhism, and Arvo Pärt's Orthodox Christianity. There's no apparent musical reason for this.

grid). Music history is a loop and a grid, in dynamic, mutually supporting motion, and minimalist music puts loop and grid together in audible dynamic and mutually supporting ways. Serialism is all grid, and close-ended. Aleatory is also all grid, but at least with Cage, each piece had a new, different grid, a series of inventions. What minimalism did was restore the conversation between past and present, the classic way of modernism to make the past both new and renewed.

History is memories, so minimalism didn't just move forward day by day, it moved in and out of music making. Riley's *In C* is the first piece of identifiable minimalism, progressing through repeated small units of music, section by section, until there's nothing left to play. But Riley quickly moved off in another direction based around his tremendous keyboard skills and his personal interest in Eastern religions, making dazzling, improvisatory music that uses repeated fast music in a mantra-like, dervish way, a la his 1972 Shanti album, *Persian Surgery Dervishes*. Morton Feldman gets roped into minimalist discussions, notably by Strickland, because of the minimal music he made in the 1950s and 1960s. That music is not minimalist, but he actually did have a minimalist period in the last ten years or so of his life. Some of his later, long-duration works, especially his String Quartet No. 2, are absolutely minimalist. They use small, cell-like musical ideas, each repeated many times then followed by a slight but clear variation on that idea, itself repeated several times. That is, the classic minimalist structural technique, music of gradual change that processes its relationship with time. Feldman has a vastly different aesthetic sense from other minimalist composers and his musical ideas were quite different in his first couple of decades composing, with dissonant, non-functional harmonies and no audible beat or even strong pulse. But in the five-hour String Quartet No. 2 he is defining time in the same way, as a flow you hear being marked and subdivided as it passes, a regular sensation that reveals the gradually shifting nature of the music. Each repetition is a brick in a larger edifice, each variation one in a slightly different shape or hue, the size of the whole accumulating through time. As this describes some of Feldman's music,[26] so it does Reich and Glass, and other minimalists, and also answers the paradox of language that often arises, that minimalist music can have maximal duration. It's all in the number of bricks.

The other part of natural history that minimalism restored was classical music's relationship to the public. Minimalism is unusually popular in the contemporary context of classical music and how it exists in consumerism and mass media, but having such a presence is normal as part of the older cycles of history. This is another thing serialism brought to a screeching halt. Serial music didn't have a relationship with the public, just other composers and new music specialists. Milton Babbitt wasn't responsible for the title of "Who Cares if You Listen?" for his essay about how contemporary music was meant for specialists,[27] both practitioners and listeners, but it got at a truth; they were speaking an arcane language to each other.

[26] The magic of Feldman is in his sensibility, which remained steady through the years even as his methods changed. String Quartet No. 2 not only can be heard like Reich and Glass, but it can be heard like Young, and even Cage.
[27] Babbitt wrote this article as "The Composer as Specialist" for *High Fidelity* magazine, and when it was published in February 1958, the editors had changed the title to the punchier but now notorious one.

Reich and Glass were doing the opposite. The classical establishment rejected them (and it's still easy to find vituperative complaints about their music among older critics and on contemporary message boards; as a clearinghouse for both you can't beat the Slipped Disc blog of British classical music journalist Norman Lebrecht, https://slippedisc.com) during their rise in the 1960s. It would take a decade or so before they could give up the last of their day jobs and support themselves solely through music, but they reached the public from the start. In the galleries and loft spaces where they gave concerts, they drew audiences from outside classical music—Tom Johnson was reviewing these, and so were writers from magazines like *Vogue*—who weren't necessarily sure what they were hearing, but knew it was new and avant-garde (without much knowing the classical tradition behind it) and that while it wasn't the rock they were used to, it had the same public-facing energy, and they wanted to hear more.

It was time for this and it was time for time in music. Culture was not only repeatable, but there had been decades of time-management studies guiding physical movement in the workplace, assembly line manufacturing, automatic record changers, the regular kathunk-kathunk-kathunk of railroad cars passing over ties, data entry jobs, cereal boxes and coffee cans laid out in aisles in the supermarket. Both Reich and Glass drove cabs for a while, and at night on 2nd Avenue in Manhattan, if you time it just right, the lights change at each intersection just as you approach, without ever changing speed they go green green green green green at regular intervals all the way down to Houston Street.

Minimalism was happening in the physical world that people knew, and it sounded like it belonged to that world. It had a beat, a regular pulse, it had rhythms. Maybe they were different from the usual, but they were there, and clear and purposeful. And that was another divide with the classical academies. Again, the story that gets told about class cal music getting to the mid-twentieth century is mostly told by people inside classical music who have the time and support to tell that story. What they see is a product of their classical training, whether that's compositional, instrumental, analytical, or historical. It is founded on both Beethoven and Bach because from the inside the story of the music is that of developments in harmony. In classical music analysis, harmony has a privileged place, it is the primary subject of music theory. Melody and rhythm, on the other hand; hardly at all. There is a bias toward harmony being the thing that conveys complexity— an unfortunate by-product of the influence of Beethoven and Bach as world historical geniuses—as artistically and intellectually superior to rhythm. This is of course nonsense, and the inability of musicology to truly quantify the genius of jazz rhythm indicates that possibly it's more sophisticated than harmony. It's also so fundamental to human music-making going back to prehistory that it's bizarre to shunt it aside in any musical analysis. It's like writing about paintings while ignoring the colors. The audible beat in minimalism may have been gauche to classical specialists, but it's a pleasure that people want to experience. In the cycles of historical time, minimalism goes back to prehistory before it starts heading to the future, and so has even deeper roots than most of the rest of classical tradition. And the audible beat marks time.

Again, this was part of minimalism restoring the path and process of classical tradition. Drums and percussion have never not been a central part to global music-making, and that includes classical music. The presence of the audible beat waxed and waned through styles and contexts—it's there in

Baroque dance music, slowly diminishes during the eighteenth and nineteenth centuries, then returns with a vengeance through Mahler, Stravinsky, the avant-garde music of Edward Varèse, Henry Cowell, and others a century ago—but it was far too pedestrian for what the academies, institutions, and even record companies thought constituted the repertoire after (and even before) the Second World War. This was another part of serialism's general break with historical time, and the application of the technique to composing was aesthetically antithetical to it.

Like with a sinkhole on a highway, the normal flow of ideas from the past into the present was broken. The minimalists were working with the present, with non-classical music that surrounded them, and the useful and inspiring past was mostly distant. The result in listening is the uncanny feeling, even sixty years later, that the music came out of nowhere as something brand new, free from history in a way serialism could only hope for. Along with its other qualities, it always sounds fresh, and attempts to connect it to pre-Second World War modernism and avant-garde music never fit. Drone music inherently feels ancient, something held in our Neanderthal DNA. Minimal music has a clear, direct connection to the slender miniatures of Erik Satie, but his *Vexations*, one single page of music meant to be played 840 times, is not an antecedent of minimalism, and Satie is very much the sound of *La Belle Époque*. Even Young has roots in his own recent past, not only atonalism but the Beatnik movement and likely the intellectual and aesthetic influence of the nearly forgotten composer Dennis Johnson. Johnson was a friend of Young's when the latter was at UCLA in the 1950s (both were friends with Terry Jennings, a talented minimal composer who fell into heroin addiction and was robbed and murdered, aged 41). Johnson made very little music and left the field in the early 1960s, but not after sketching out a monumental piano piece, *November*, and recording a cassette of it. In 2013, the Irritable Hedgehog label released a four-and-a-half-hour reconstruction put together by Kyle Gann that shows the influence Young always acknowledged from Johnson for his own long-duration, minimal, *The Well-Tuned Piano*, his supreme masterpiece.

Drone music had roots, minimal music had roots. Minimalism seems to spring spontaneously from the head of Zeus. And while that's not true, it likely seemed like it in late fall in San Francisco, 1964.

3 Minimalist Music

In the scope of cultural history, there are infinitesimally few examples of when everything changed in a single moment. When Beethoven's Symphony No. 3 premiered in Vienna, April 7, 1805, the romantic era of classical music began. The same thing happened on November 4, 1964, when Terry Riley and musicians began playing *In C* at the San Francisco Tape Music Center (he was one of the founders, along with Ramon Sender and Morton Subotnick) at 321 Divisadero Street. The ensemble was packed with some of the premier names in avant-garde and experimental music: Steve Reich played the electric organ; Pauline Oliveros played the accordion; Subotnick played the clarinet; and Jon Gibson (who was to become one of the most important musicians in the Philip Glass Ensemble and a minimalist composer in his own right) played saxophone.

In C is a piece for any number of different instruments. They all have the same music, a series of fifty-three discrete and small (some are only one note) ideas that are played and repeated before the musicians move on to the next, in sequence from 1 to 53. This is a modular form that composers had been exploring since the 1950s with pieces like Pierre Boulez' Piano Sonata No. 3, which is organized in several sections the performer can put in the order they choose each time they play it, or *FOLIO* and *Four Systems* composed by Cage's colleague Earle Brown, a set of graphic scores that can also have their order rearranged. *In C* modules, on the other hand, are meant to work in sequence. Though the tempo is usually quick, the music itself isn't very hard to play, easily within reach of amateurs. It's the repetition that makes it special and groundbreaking. In the performing directions, Riley instructs:

#

> Patterns are to be played consecutively with each performer having the freedom to determine how many times he or she will repeat each pattern before moving on to the next. There is no fixed rule as to the number of repetitions a pattern may have, however, since performances normally average between 45 minutes and an hour and a half, it can be assumed that one would repeat each pattern from somewhere between 45 seconds and a minute and a half or longer …
>
> Each pattern can be played in unison or canonically in any alignment with itself or with its neighboring patterns. One of the joys of *IN C* is the interaction of the players in polyrhythmic combinations that spontaneously arise between patterns. Some quite fantastic shapes will arise and disintegrate as the group moves through the piece when it is properly played.
>
> It is important not to hurry from pattern to pattern but to stay on a pattern long enough to interlock with other patterns being played. As the performance progresses, performers should stay within 2 or 3 patterns of each other. It is important not to race too far ahead or to lag too far behind.

(Riley had the score printed and distributed inside the original 1968 recording from Columbia. It's been freely available for decades on the internet, and the Third Coast Percussion ensemble hosts the score, with transpositions for instruments in different keys, at https://thirdcoastpercussion.com/terry-rileys-in-c/.)

#

What this sounds like is a shimmering sonic stew of bright, warm textures, no matter the instrumentation. This is major key music, always consonant, and since playing it requires the musicians to listen to each other and work together in a consensus, it's impossible to play it without a glowing community spirit and real joy. This is the first minimalist statement, and Riley was the first minimalist composer.

Or maybe it's better to see him as the first composer to make minimalist music, because he didn't mean to be a minimalist and didn't remain so. *In C* for him wasn't about exploring the possibilities of the process of gradual change through time— he didn't even have the on-the-beat pulse that opens the piece and runs through it, that's something Reich suggested to him in rehearsals to help keep everyone organized. He was interested in spiritual practice and altered perceptions through music. He told minimalist composer William Duckworth:

\#

… music was also able to transport us suddenly out of one reality into another. Transport us so that we would a most be having visions as we were playing. So that's what I was thinking about before I wrote *In C*. I believe music, shamanism, and magic are all connected, and when it's used that way it creates the most beautiful use of music.[1]

\#

After *In C*, Riley continued to make heavily repetitive music, but it's not minimalist but mantra-maximalism. The shaman feeling in it is visceral and makes Riley a beloved figure who bridges the worlds of classical, jazz, and non-Western music. *In C* is the indispensable "first dream, first poetic" outcry of minimalism, even if Riley was an accidental minimalist.

[1] William Duckworth, *Talking Music* (New York: Schirmer Books, 1995), 269.

Accidents will happen. History is full of them. Minimalist music exists because of two particular ones. That's not to say that it began purely by chance, but that, as Louis Pasteur said, chance favors the prepared mind, and both Reich and Glass were prepared to take full advantage of experiences they never expected. For Reich, the accident happened in the electronic music studio.

Even though he played in the *In C* premiere, neither Reich nor anyone at the time showed any notion of what had just happened. They played an intriguing experiment in repetitive music and modular form and then they went on to other things (Oliveros and her "deep listening" ideas, Subotnick as one of the great electronic music composers). Reich was exploring ideas around using tape and delay systems that he had picked up from Riley, and one day in 1964 recorded street preacher Brother Walter sermonizing about the end of the world in Union Square, San Francisco (this was soon enough after the Cuban Missile Crisis that Brother Walter, Reich, and many others had nuclear annihilation at the front of their minds). Back in the studio, Reich duplicated and looped part of the recording, then played it on two different tape machines. They were out of sync with each other, and the loops started to move in and out of phase. What Reich heard was a gradual process of movement and transformation, based on repeated patterns, and produced the results as *It's Gonna Rain* (with the original extended title of: *or meet Brother Walter in Union Square after listening to Terry Riley*), and the rest has literally been history.

This was the start of Reich's period of "phase" compositions, which began with the tape loop pieces and ran through *Drumming* (1970–1), one of his great masterpieces and a culmination of this original exploration of music as a gradual process. The phase pieces were ones written for instruments so that the phenomenon he heard in the studio could be performed live. The prime examples are *Piano Phase*, for two pianos (or two marimbas) and *Violin Phase*, for solo violin playing against a tape, or four violins playing live, and the more conceptual *Pendulum Music*. In his *Conversations* book, Reich explains phasing to artist Richard Serra as, "one performer gets slightly faster than the other and slowly moves ahead a sixteenth—just by accelerating a little bit … And that's the phasing process."[2] In the phase pieces, two (or more parts) start in unison, then one starts to push slightly forward in time, setting up a shimmering phase differential sound between them, before they come back into unison again, all the while their repeated patterns are moving forward through time. The music is simple, a set of riffs that just repeat, everything staying on the same chord. As the parts move in and out of phase, all sorts of relationships form and gradually slide away into others; sometimes there's the sound of one instrument echoing another, then there are moments when it sounds like one is in counterpoint with the other, or continuing a line the other picks up and extends. All the while, they're passing through each other, a constant process of gradual shifts. The music plays until it stops, it doesn't go anywhere except where time takes it, but it's always in motion and transforming from one state to the next. This is Reich at his most hardcore, which may seem forbidding on paper but these pieces are hypnotic to hear and

---

2   At the Whitney Museum in 1969, Serra and artists Bruce Nauman and Michael Snow, and composer James Tenney released the mikes for *Pendulum Music* for the exhibition for which Reich wrote "Music as a Gradual Process" for the catalog. Pérotin returns as a property of physics, with each mike swing slowing/augmenting as directed by the loss of angular momentum.

especially to see performed, full of psychoacoustic effects that have the listener's imagination chasing sounds that may or may not be there. They also have something of the abyss in them, illustrating the time that is passing for all of us and that will never return. A fifteen-minute performance of *Violin Phase* is fifteen enthralling minutes of hearing fifteen minutes or your life pass by. Why not fill it with music?

The phase pieces culminate with *Drumming*. This is one of the heights of his career and a piece that marks the turning point of the end of the phasing style and into a less conceptual and more concrete minimalist compositional technique. *Drumming* is also a substantial step from the phase pieces, still using that experimental method but now as a device to get from one point to the next rather than just complete in itself. The duration is longer too, from about an hour to eighty minutes, depending on the tempo and number of repeats the musicians take.

There's an enormously vital social aspect as well. Reich had spent time in 1970 in Ghana, studying African drumming. He learned by following the teacher, playing the lesson back until he had gotten it right, then moving on to the next. Part of that he applied to *Drumming*, as Russell Hartenberger remembered from the rehearsals:

#

The thing that struck me about it was that I was also starting African Drumming and Gamelan at Wesleyan. And it was exactly how I was being taught those musics. Just imitation and repetition, the teacher would show me something and I would just play it until I got it, and then we would move along. It was curious that here was a piece of western music by a traditional western composer, being taught in the same way that I was learning non-Western Music.[3]

#

Drumming is about minimalism and phasing again, about how music gradually changes in time while showing time passing, and it's about something more: musicians working together to make the music happen. In this and Reich's other large ensemble masterpiece, *Music for 18 Musicians*, the musicians have to listen to and cue each other, keep track of musical moments that signal what comes next, and frequently share not just instruments but physical space as one passes the part to another without missing a note. What *Drumming* gets at is how music-making is a social activity. That's at the core of non-Western music like African drumming and gamelan, which Reich would also study before *Music for 18 Musicians*, the integration between playing an instrument and playing it in cooperation with other musicians as a community. Reich didn't make the music to tell a story, he did it to establish a process that he and his musicians would work out together. There's great human drama in seeing this in action.

And the sound is just beautiful. This is the start of Reich orchestrating more carefully and imaginatively. Percussion is the core, and it's always pitched in one way or another, from piano to vibraphone to marimba, even tuned bongos, and he adds the brightness of woodwinds and soprano voices, and sometimes has the drummers express vocal sounds when they strike the instruments. Things are always thwacking or ringing

---

[3]   Steve Reich, *Conversations* (Toronto: Hanover Square, 2022), 104.

or even whistling, and the constant activity creates a lot of psychoacoustic images.

Drumming is an extraordinary work, so is *Music for 18 Musicians*, which followed in 1974. This is his most famous piece, well-known due to the ECM album of the same title released in 1978. There's a real before-and-after shift in Reich's work after *Drumming*. The phasing is gone, replaced by a focus on sharper rhythms and syncopations, exact phrases, the music not flowing through itself but working in synchronization to build things in time, and then shift them forward. Phasing was an experiment in the possibilities of process music, *Music for 18 Musicians* is a consolidation of everything that Reich learned into a way of composing that is the classical music of today, taking methods and styles from Bach and Stravinsky, combining them with what's in contemporary culture, and making music that became the touchstone for both his contemporary peers who were attracted to minimalism and the following generations of composers.

Before Glass started writing symphonies, this felt like the minimalist symphony. The piece cycles through a series of loosely connected chords that act as an introduction, and later a conclusion. It then moves through eleven sections—transitions are cued by a series of chords from the vibraphone—and there's a constant shimmer of eighth notes. Some of the sections are for the ensemble to play everything together, others keep up the pulse under a solo piano or marimba. All the thematic material is in minimalist method, starting with one note that repeats, then it's two, then three, then five, each time building up to almost a fully looping phrase, but always moving on to the next. Completely immersive and gorgeous, this is one of the great compositions in classical music, of any era, and has had a central place in the history and continued life of minimalism.

#

Glass is well-described by Richard Kostelanetz as "the most visible sometime-avant-garde composer of his generation."[4] The first part was certainly true when that was written in the late 1990s, but it's possible that John Williams has eclipsed Glass in terms of public visibility, and in any given year this century Arvo Pärt is the most-performed living composer. But the popularity is far less meaningful than the second part, which is a succinct way to cover the cirection of Glass's composing across a span of over fifty years. After some very early works in an unformed style that touched on dissonance and post-Schoenberg modernism that still held onto romantic, communicative aspirations, the roots of minimalism came to him through the combination of chance and epiphany.

In the mid-1960s Glass was living in Paris, studying technique with Nadia Boulanger (the most important music teacher of the twentieth century and possibly in the history of Western music; some of her dozens of students were Copland, Burt Bacharach, Errol Morris—who as a documentary filmmaker has hired Glass for multiple scores—Elliott Carter, Astor Piazzolla, and Quincy Jones), and getting involved in making music for theater. Through a friend, he got a gig helping with the music production for a film Conrad Rooks was directing, *Chappaqua*. In one of the uncanny moments of crossed-paths in cultural history, Ornette Coleman had already recorded a score for the movie (released in 1966 by Columbia as *Chappaqua Suite*). In his memoir, *Words without Music*, Glass tells how Rooks played

---

[4] Richard Kostelanetz, ed., *Writings on Glass: Essays, Interviews, Criticism* (New York: Schirmer, 1997), vii.

Coleman's score, which Glass thought was "a masterpiece," but the director wanted something different. He asked Ravi Shankar, already the international star of Indian classical music, to score the film—as a weird and confused collision of beatnik and hippie drug culture, perhaps Rooks thought the kids were more into the sound of the sitar. This was Glass's introduction to Shankar—they would reunite in 1990 to make the studio album *Passages*—and, essentially, music outside the Western tradition.

Glass confesses he was ignorant of non-Western music, and writes, "At my first listening I couldn't make heads or tails of it." His job was to sit with Shankar in the studio while the latter improvised in the Indian tradition to the film, writing down the music and notating it[5] for a small instrumental ensemble to play. Through this work, and especially with the guidance and insight of Shankar's tabla player, Alla Rakha, Glass discovered an entirely new way to organize rhythms and melodic phrases outside of the standard meters and bar lines of Western music. As a very rough example, instead of the music's time being organized by a common four beats to a bar, and smaller divisions within each beat, it was set out in a sixteen-beat pattern. That revelation, and the working practice of writing out one part for one instrument at a time instead of the typical one of composing a full score in a vertical array and separating out individual parts later, was the beginning of a new style.

And at the beginning, the style was avant-garde. That term and "experimental" are tossed around promiscuously when it comes to discussing new music that doesn't fit into expected

---

[5] This is a skill learned through ear training, a basic component of the practice commonly termed and little understood as "classical training."

forms, but they mean two different things. Experimental music is made without a predetermined outcome, and an integral part of it is discovering just what will happen—Reich using phasing. Avant-garde music takes a central idea and pushes it as far as it can possibly go. A useful understanding where that places such movements, and what Reich and Glass did for classical music, comes from T.S. Eliot in his important essay "Tradition and the Individual Talent." Though writing about poetry his idea that new ideas and work can stretch away from the tradition that is their context, but never detach and eventually become the new frontier that future artists will continue to pull further, applies to every creative art.

Avant-garde music does that stretching and pulling (experimental music can as well, but that's not the main purpose), and Glass did just that as an avant-garde composer. Starting with patterns of beats, he explored how far they could go and still work. Or even not work. The influence of Reich's music on him turned him away from dissonance to the basic consonance of major and minor tonality, and he played around with an additive/subtractive process—repeating a simple musical idea and gradually adding more notes and new accents to it, or taking some away—in pieces like *Music in the Shape of a Square* (1968), and *Two Pages* and *Music in Fifths* (both 1969). The latter two are rigorous, at the extreme edge of Glass's process. Even played with a multi-instrument ensemble instead of just piano, there's a challenge and a severity that, depending on mood and circumstances, can push these pieces into exercises in the endurance of both performer and listener.

That was the point at which Glass, with his technique and materials etched down to a precise, firm set, established the new minimalist frontier of the classical tradition and expanded it from there. The great works from this period are *Music in Twelve Parts* and *Einstein on the Beach*. *Einstein* has a substantial reputation, and even though it requires a lot of patience to simply wait for a time when there's a new production, and patience for its five-hour duration, it launched his career as a prolific and important opera composer. Glass is upfront about this in a way that cements him as a great keeper of the long and deep classical tradition. In his memoir, after he explains that he tells people he's a theater composer, he writes:

#

> That is actually what I do, and what I have done. That doesn't meant that's the only thing I ever did … You only need to look at the history of music: the big changes come in the opera house. It happened with Monteverdi … It happened with Mozart … Wagner … and Stravinsky. The theater suddenly puts the composer in an unexpected relationship to his work … Once you get into the world of theater and you're referencing all its elements—movement, image, text, and music—unexpected things can take place. The composer then finds himself … in a situation where he doesn't know what to do. If you don't know what to do, there's actually a chance of doing something new.[6]

#

Einstein, which premiered in 1976, made him famous, though not enough to turn him into a full-time composer. He and director Robert Wilson raised the money and produced the touring performances themselves—they rented the Metropolitan Opera House—and went deeply into debt, and

---

[6] Philip Glass, *Words without Music: A Memoir* (New York: Liveright, 2015), 128–9.

Glass (who had started a moving company with Reich, drove a cab, and did some basic plumbing work) was still holding down day jobs when he was composing his next opera, *Satyagraha*. There was no recording of *Einstein* available until 1978, so more people knew about it then knew it, and things like the headline for Clive Barnes review in *The New York Times*, "'Einstein on the Beach' Transforms Boredom into Memorable Theater" (November 23, 1976), easily trigger thoughts of an *enfant terrible* of the avant-garde. But as *Music in Twelve Parts* shows, and the opera *Satyagraha* would cement, even though Glass was wielding an avant-garde compositional process with formidable skill, he was then a classical composer.

Music in Twelve Parts doesn't have nearly the same public profile, and it has nothing to do with the theater or Glass not knowing what to do. Quite the opposite, it's something of an ideal presentation of all the things Glass did know in the middle-1970s, a piece that demonstrates all his ideas and techniques, and also the sound and feeling he values It's the single most important composition he's made.

Music in Twelve Parts was composed between 1971 and 1974 and had its premiere performance at the Town Hall on West 43rd Street in Manhattan on June 1. Like Glass's very beginnings as a minimalist composer, the piece was also something of an accident. He had written what is now "Part 1," a gorgeous, languid stream of flowing, cyclically repetitive polyphony and counterpoint, and played it for a friend, saying the title was "Music in Twelve Parts," because there were twelve individual musical lines. Fernando González related the story in the program notes for the 50th anniversary performance of the complete work, in Town Hall, May 25, 2025, of how when it was done Glass's friend said, "That's very beautiful, what are the other eleven parts going to be like?" Glass thought that was "an interesting misunderstanding," and decided to write eleven more "Parts."

Written in the individual-voice style that had come out of his work with Shankar and using his specialist group The Philip Glass Ensemble—with Glass himself playing one of the keyboards—this is the central work in his career. It is a culmination of his thinking from the first day in the recording studio for *Chappaqua* up through the preceding avant-garde experiments and is a catalog of what he had learned and also, intriguingly, what was to come. The twelve parts are individual modules that can be played in sequence (with necessary breaks for rest) in a whole concert, which takes about four-and-a-half hours, or else played separately and/or in different combinations. There's no structural relationship between them, they only connect in the way the musicians segue immediately from the end of one to the start of the next.

In the piece, Glass takes his repetitive-additive technique and makes it polyphonic; there's not just one repeated line (that may or may not be played in parallel octaves) but several, each working in counterpoint with the others and building flowing harmonies and polyrhythms. The sound is modern, with Glass's signature combination of reedy organ and saxophone and clear, pealing flute and voice, and everything is on the same plane, with no soloists or lead voices. This is ensemble music, and despite the instrumentation is very close to Renaissance choral music, full of passages that come directly out of Mozart's tradition, and put together in a large-scale form that is just one step past the grand nineteenth-century symphonies of Anton Bruckner (himself an avant-gardist *avant la lettre*.) The music is a template for what was to come for many years, with specific devices he would reuse in later pieces—he would take Part 11 and Part 12 and with alterations use them with central purpose and effect in *Einstein*. It's also a venture into just how far and deep minimalism could go in processing and shaping time.

Glass wrote his own note to the audience in the original program:

#

It was my intention to confront directly the problem of musical scale (or time). The music is placed outside the usual time-scale, substituting a non-narrative and extended time-sense in its place. It may happen that some listeners, missing the usual musical structures (or landmarks) by which they are used to orient themselves, may experience some in tial difficulties in actually perceiving the music. However, when it becomes apparent that nothing "happens" in the usual sense, but that, instead, the gradual accretion of musical material can and does serve as the basis of the listener's attention, then he can perhaps discover another mode of listening—one in which neither memory nor anticipation (the usual psychological devices of programmatic music whether Baroque, Classical, Romantic or Modernistic) have a place in sustaining the texture, quality or reality of the musical experience.

He also writes a concise and informative explanation of the methods and style he was using at the time:

#

Certain principles remain constant in *Music in 12* [*sic*] *Parts*—a stable harmony, repetitive structures and a steady eighth-note beat. Additive process (in which a simple melodic figure is altered after a number of repetitions by the addition or subtraction of one or a group of related notes) is used throughout, though often combined with principles of cyclic rhythmic structures (a device familiar in a number of non-Western traditions).

However, the individual parts … tend to be highly divergent from each other, exhibiting a range as wide as I could conceive of at the time of writing.

A view of the work as a whole would have to take into account these two rather contradictory tendencies. In any case, the question of whether *Music in 12 Parts* is an organic whole or a collection of distinct pieces may prove to be irrelevant— that is, if, as I suspect, the musical personality of the composer is in fact the fundamental unifying principle of the music.[7]

#

That last may be the defining difference between the styles of Reich and Glass. The former values a kind of warm diffidence, an attractive and outward-reaching sound that doesn't try to express any emotional experience, while the latter has a classic, old-school sense of being a composer, expressing their personality through sound and style. That's the epitome of the romantic musical artist.

Even *Einstein*, with its discontinuous and mostly spoken-word libretto, the haunting choruses repeatedly singing "One two three four / One two three four five six / One two three four five six seven eight"—they are telling you the number of beats they're singing on, as if Shankar were singing his raga pattern— the long and arpeggiated violin soliloquies, is recognizably classical music that is being used to make a music drama. That drama might be meant for contemporary avant-garde and experimental theater sensibilities, but that's Wilson's domain,

---

[7] PDF of the original program for *Music in Twelve Parts* provided by The Town Hall.

while the elegant, sophisticated, and powerful harmonic modulations in the "Train" scene in Act 1 and "Spaceship" in Act 4 are as fundamentally classical, and operatic, as it gets.

What is *Einstein on the Beach* about? It is the science portion of a trilogy finished through *Satyagraha*—about Gandhi and politics—and *Akhnaten*—about the pharaoh who temporarily established monotheism, and so about religion—but that needs more precision. With scenes that are built around trains and spaceships, *Einstein* dramatizes Albert Einstein's breakthroughs, including his famous thought experiment imaging what someone on a train might see compared to someone standing still on the side of the tracks. That was a way for Einstein to explain his ideas about how velocity through space affected the flow of time. Fundamentally, then, the opera is about time, as described by musical processes. There it is again, music that is about how time works and about how music works in time, used to portray a drama about thinking about how time works, how it's related to space, how those two things come together to form and alter our experience of time, which itself is produced by the universe's expansion into space, which creates every future moment in which music can develop, where each next note goes.

These are not things that anyone needs to think about when listening to Glass or any other minimalist music, but that these things are the very material of minimalism itself, that connect the genre more directly to the basic existence of the universe than most any other manner or form of art, are inherent to its pull.

Reich and Glass deserve heavy focus because they are the two most consequential minimalist composers. It is their work that has both shown the way forward for minimalism and the classical tradition as a whole, and the enormous distance in style between the two shows how rich and varied minimalism and its influence is. Another minimalist who has been praised but never given her due as an essential and foundational figure who is also defining the range of minimalism is Meredith Monk.

First, a digression—minimalist music is an embodiment of time that plays out in the physical performances of musicians. Seeing this live means seeing time represented through the motion of bodies. This isn't something that the minimalists meant to do (with one exception), but it is a manifestation of how the music works—it can't be helped, for which, eternal gratitude. To go back to Reich's "Music as a Gradual Process," this is process music and for it to be minimalism the listener has to hear the process working—seeing this live is like watching a marvelous, gigantic (or small!) human machine, musicians not just playing together but working together. As great as it is to listen to *Drumming* or *Music for 18 Musicians* on your stereo, there is nothing like witnessing a live performance and seeing how the musicians work together in space, coordinating handing off parts from one to the other; or two percussionist facing each other across a set of marimbas sharing a rhythmic pattern by having one play the downbeat and the other the upbeat; to watch them cue and coordinate with each other; to appreciate the physical effort and concentration involved in shaking a set of maracas for several minutes, non-stop, without missing a beat. There is great power in seeing what goes into producing such glorious sounds.

Reich has had a mostly indirect but profound partnership with dancer and choreographer Anna Theresa de Keersmaeker. She has made dances to several of his compositions, including *Drumming*, for which the dancing is surprisingly lyrical and even funny. Her piece *Fase*, from 1982, is a collection of dances to four of his early works, *Piano Phase, Come Out, Violin Phase*, and *Clapping Music.* She represents the phasing process through dance, and this is particularly fascinating in *Piano Phase*, with two dancers whirling in place with one arm extended on the horizontal, coordinated in time. As the two pianos in the music move in and out of phase with each other on the way to flowing into new musical phrases, so too do the dancers offset from each other in time, even as they follow the same choreography in space. Seeing this makes the music and its process even clearer. A review of a 2021 performance in Germany touched on the human-working-time-as-a-machine aspect the choreography writes out in space, "One seldom-discussed fact about the origin of Reich's phase music is that it is 'indigenous to machines,'"[8] pointing out how Reich's technique came out of hearing the same tape loop moving in and out of synchronicity on two misaligned tape machines (*It's Gonna Rain*). The accident of a machine's malfunction has led to sixty years of astonishing music.

The exception noted above is Meredith Monk. Born five years after Glass, six after Reich, and seven after Riley, she's from the same generation but came to minimalist music from a different path than those three. Riley at his core is a practicing and performing musician, Reich and Glass are composers, Monk is a multi-disciplinary artist who studied music and dance at Sarah Lawrence College in the 1960s, but whose artistic essence goes back to learning Dalcroze Eurhythmics as a child. That is a fascinating program where music is integrated in every way into physical movement. If someone is playing a piano or a drum, everyone else is moving in time to the music, and when you sing, you move your body along with

[8] Rathsaran Sireekan, "Man as Machine: A Journey Back into Phase Shifting," *Rosas*, June 14, 2021. https://www.rosas.be/en/news/882-man-as-machine-a-journey-back-into-phase-shifting.

the notes and sounds—this can be as simple as bending at the waist while singing a downward scale. The point is that music is embodied in every way, and this clearly dug itself into Monk's synapses and bones. She told *The Guardian* in 2022 that it "influenced everything I've done. It's why dance and movement and film are so integral to my music. It's why I see music so visually."[9]

Musically, Monk is a minimalist, one of the great ones and one of the important ones. Her compositional style is something of a middle ground between Reich and Glass, she likes the smaller, transparent sound of Reich's scoring (though with darker woodwinds) while using a technique that's more of Glass' additive process. The main thing though is that her music is meant first and foremost for performance, for seeing her and her musicians (like her colleagues she has run her own specialized ensemble for decades) moving together in coordination with each other and the music, and their bodies moving in response to what and how they are singing.

The voice and body are central to her work. Reich and Glass discovered the possibilities of process music and established minimalism through happy accidents. Monk had her own, as she explains: "Sometime in the mid-1960s, as I was vocalizing in my studio, I suddenly had a revelation that the voice could have the same flexibility and range of movement as a spine or a foot,"[10] and found that minimalism was the ideal vehicle

[9]   John Lewis, "Interview: 'I feel like an aesthetic mother to Björk'—the amazing Meredith Monk on composing with growls, gasps, chirrups and yodels,'" *The Guardian*, March 22, 2022. https://www.theguardian.com/music/2022/mar/22/meredith-monk-composer-performer-bjork-voice.

[10] Anna Schneider, ed., *Meredith Monk Calling* (Berlin: Hate Cantz, 2024), 49.

to support the movement of the voice. Without intending, her style makes her arguably the first post-minimalist composer, even as minimalism was still developing. and she is unique in how her music marks and describes the passage of time while also exploring the uncanny spiritual depths of human experience that La Monte Young and Terry Riley—after *In* C-do. Everything is rooted in her body and those of her performers, and everything is rooted in song as intuitively and immediately understood by the listener.

She mainly realizes her ideas in songs and theater works, and the former are components of the latter. Her theater is a great realization of *gesamtkuntswerk*, a hazy and overused concept invented by Carl Friedrich Eusebius Trahndorff and furthered by Richard Wagner. In a technocratic age, it's become a shorthand for using multiple tools of stagecraft, which has been standard practice in the theater for centuries. Monk is one of the exceedingly few artists who have realized this idea of integrating multiple arts into a whole. Because all her work is an expression of what happens in the body it seems too intuitive to fit with a philosophical ideal, but that's precisely why her complete, seamless, and organic mix of thought, singing, instrumental music, and physical movement coordinated with each preceding element and among performers—in and through time—is a compete demonstration of the possibilities of a total art work. And by being a minimalist, she also turns everything into the material of time.

Also, in her own way, she understands Newman's concept of aesthetic expression as fundamental to being human, "I was interested in primordial utterance: what were the first human sounds? What was the delicate … membrane between speech and music?"[11] That gives her music a tremendous naturalness,

---

[11]   Ibid, 49.

the quality of something that emerges as easily and normally as breathing and walking. The simplest details set her apart from everyone else; one of the most basic things that happen in her performances is that the vocalists, and often some instrumentalists too, walk around while singing. The effect is extraordinary, cementing the reality that making music is a social activity and a physical activity into something that feels monumental and profound (it is profound), and also elevating every element of her music, no matter how prosaic or vernacular, to a sophisticated, abstract level of structure and form. She's one step beyond from Reich when it comes to the physical embodiment of his compositions, not just seeing performers work together to realize the music but following them as they move through space, integrating instrumental music, voice, dance, composition, and choreography into a visual depiction of the music. And like Keersmaeker's choreography, Monk visually marks the passing time in a duplication of how her music does the same—it is not just multimedia but multidimensional.

She is a superb composer in the classical sense, with roots that are even deeper in that tradition than Reich and Glass. By working out of the body and how it moves and sings, she starts from a point that precedes even the roots of the European classical tradition. Her fantastic *Dolmen Music* and *Do You Be?* albums put her in the minimalist mix, wordless vocal fantasias of glossolalia and physical music-making over repeating patterns and cadences that could be mistaken for one of the "Knee Plays" from *Einstein*. There are moments in her music, like "Acts From Under And Above: Scared Songs," where the sung trills and chirps and yelps turn into words. These are more intriguing and exciting parallels to the physical universe, a model in sound of how virtual particles are constantly emerging from and collapsing back into the vacuum of space.

Her opera *Atlas* is the great avant-garde, minimalist opera, in a way that *Einstein* is not. It is a radical work in gentle clothing, like everything else she does, that starts with the fundamental practice of how humans create music and ends up as something that might be the most successful realization of the ideal of a universal language that communicates across every culture and experience. Glass's is part of his musical restoration of ideas from classical harmony—it's formally abstract from the perspective of drama and theater, but musically it's one of his steps along the path to becoming the great classical composer of his era. *Atlas* is minimalism in its purest form and sense, and the context of a drama shows how Monk's folk music roots bring out music that has such naturalness it seems spontaneous, and accessible in the way that it seems almost anyone from the audience could just join in the singing and even the movement. And it has virtually no words, which is Monk's method; wordless vocal sounds, things like trills, yodeling, "la-la-las," glossolalia, and the like. Rather than making her music hermetic or obscure, it makes it deeply communicative, the notes and the performers telling you everything you need to know through pitch, sound, and gesture. As powerful as it is to see musicians playing *Drumming*, a Monk ensemble performance goes far beyond.

Atlas is absolutely an opera in every sense of the word, originating from and embedded in that tradition. Perhaps it's possible to say that opera is something closely related to classical music but its own, slightly independent genre. That doesn't exclude Monk's minimalism from classical music, though, rather it shows how minimalism can bring in so many other musics while remaining a clear genre (and again, except for the strange mid-twentieth-century stretch, classical music has always worked with the vernacular music in the societies and eras in which it's developed—one of the features of Glass's *Akhnaten* is that it has almost no libretto and is sung in archaic languages like Akkadian and Biblical Hebrew, while the narration and the one aria are in the vernacular of the audience wherever it is performed).

Monk's "Fear and Loathing in Gotham: Gotham Lullaby," which can be heard on her *Dolmen Music* album, is a modest-sized piece of music that has a huge effect. There's a simple, repeated, minor key pattern, her wordless singing ranges from gentle melodies to phrases that come close to what Diamanda Galas and Nina Hagen do, it's soothing and comforting like a lullaby should be but also full of the experience of urban frictions and maybe even night terrors. Even more than *Atlas*, this is music that is the "primordial utterance," sounds that come from the soul and manifest through the body as vocalizations. She is communicating from insider herself, and also showing the communicative power of repetition in music. It's not about repeating something in order to make it insistent, it's establishing a pattern and repeating it so that the listener can understand the vocabulary and grammar of what to them might be a new language.

Considered just as a listening and watching experience, Monk's work is stunning, some of the most beautiful and beautifully humane music there is. In terms of looking at minimalism as a genre, it not only is within it but invaluable to defining its qualities and scope. The idea that complicated and knotty, even incomprehensible, sounds are the sign of something more sophisticated and advanced than what the listener knows or can even grasp is a very, very hard one to let go of. If minimalism shows that music that is consonant and transparent about its workings is as sophisticated and advanced as a pre-engineered sequence of twelve notes run through first year composition class technique of permutations, then Monk and the utter simplicity of her materials is even more proof. The notes on the page look like they make children's music, and detractors of minimalism can look at that and proclaim the genre simplistic, boring, meaningless. A superficial complicatedness or difficulty can hide a lack of interesting thinking, and even good technique. There is nothing to hide behind in simplicity, the ideas and means are out in the open and demand thought, conviction, and skill. When musicians and singers play those Monk's notes, the result is a folk-minimalism, music that has the vast, complex expression of the earth under our feet, the luminous brilliance of the stars in the sky, and the mind-boggling sophistication of uniting the sounds, the scores, and the body. There's an extraordinary scene in *Atlas*, "Personal Climate: Changing Companions," where the travelers come together with the few actual words in the libretto (at one point, a character says "I am a good cook," and it's so prosaic and ordinary that it might make you weep), singing and movement. It's a representation of how music is at the foundation of civilization, how becoming *Homo aestheticus* meant that, with music, people could communicate with each other without shared language. Newness made with the most ancient means, music cannot possibly be more sophisticated or profound. That is what she adds to the genre.

#

The serialists's hearts were sort of in the right place. They wanted an international style after seeing the destruction of nationalism. That's a fine goal, but something like that has to start organically, built from the ground up through the common musical ideas that tie together people all over the globe. Serialism obviously is not that, and the serialists were something like a political cadre forcing through a vanguard from the top down, Leninists who thought they were proletarians, and one that most people just didn't want. While Faulkner was right about music and other culture, Santayana got it right with political power, at least from the standpoint of those with the power who feel compelled and justified in forcing it on others.

While there probably will never be one single international style, common everywhere, minimalism shows how that might come to be. Leave aside the conceptual aspects of the music in the context of the classical tradition and think about the sound, the playing. There's a reason that Reich studied African drumming and gamelan music, because he was doing what they do, which is organizing an ensemble music through rhythm, making music with a strong beat and pulse at the core, and putting together layers of rhythmic patterns. His instrumentation often is just wood, metal, and skins. That is the same for millennia of global music. Riley and Monk have some of those qualities too, and *In C* is played all over the world, but Reich makes his music that way people have made theirs, almost everywhere, for almost all time.[12] This isn't the West looking at the world and lumping everything into "World Music"—Reich makes music that's part of the world.

Part of the world, while also decidedly American. Like jazz, minimalism is one of this country's indigenous cultural

---

[12] He has two small, fine pieces that everyone can play, *Clapping Music* and *Music for Pieces of Wood*. All they take are hands or clave sticks, globally available resources.

creations, Reich and Monk in particular mix together the urban and rural flavors of classical music that hint at both Stravinsky and Aaron Copland. With that, and culture being such an enormous American export last century, minimalism has had an international reach. Arguably, La Monte Young's path has had even broader influence, with profound impact in places like Italy and Japan, but again that's minimal music, not minimalism in the terms of this study. Minimalist composers in other countries have been important to the genre, and one of the greatest minimalist compositions comes from Europe. These are some of the key figures:

#

Louis Andriessen (1939–2021): Andriessen was a Dutch composer who had a similar path to those of his peers, working his way through and against serialism, tape music, and the other main twentieth-century trends. Like Reich he was influence by jazz and Stravinsky, and when he first heard Reich's music he organized performances of it. His own compositional method was less process-based and more sectional, packed with repetition and polyrhythms, straddling the minimalist and post-minimalist eras. He liked his music and politics strong and loud, he used electric guitars and basses, and created an ensemble called De Volharding (Perseverance) that could march in the street and performed standing shoulder to shoulder. One of his first minimalist works, *De Staat* (*The State*), is also his most important. It's aggressive music, not as heavy as metal but even more prodding, an allegory on Plato that isn't always clear but is always insistent. He was also one of the most important composition teachers of the post-Second World War era. He taught in Europe and America, and his students include British minimalist composers Graham Fitkin and Steve Martland, Bang on a Can composer Julia Wolfe, and Missy Mazzoli, one of the stars of the current American generation.

#

Michael Nyman (born 1944): The other name in minimalist film composers is Nyman (and he's been an important critic, as has been seen). He wrote the scores for eleven of Peter Greenaway's movies, including *The Draughtman's Contract*, *The Cook, The Thief, His Wife, Her Lover*, and *Prospero's Books*. He also scored Jane Campion's *The Piano*, an award-winning international hit and a movie that, for him, spawned multiple versions and recordings of the music and broad recognition. Nyman knows American minimalism inside and out, he's been a frequent interlocutor with Reich especially and played with Reich's ensemble in England. Like Reich, he was also influenced by early music, but in his case it's the English Renaissance composer John Dowland (really one of the great singer-songwriters, but a classical composer because his music is old). Nyman's style is very European, very British, he eschewed world music ideas for material that came from Europe. There's an almost clichéd Englishness to his music that has great charm, the feeling of skiffle and dancehall music in the way he uses his instruments to give a pumping sound to his repetitive patterns and rhythms.

#

Simeon ten Holt (1923–2012): He's not the most prominent minimalist composer, but ten Holt—another Dutchman—has an important place in the music because his *Canto Ostinato* is one of the greatest works in the genre. He mostly wrote for the piano, and that's the main instrumentation for this 1976 work (it can be played, like many of Reich's pieces, on any pitched percussion instrument). It uses the modular idea of *In C* in the way it's laid out in a series of sections that are played in sequence, the musicians deciding how many times to repeat each before moving on. But the music is very different, more like Reich but still individual. There is a hypnotic repeated five-note pattern in the bass (the "ostinato"), with lines gradually coming in on top. The process is in the layers, the harmonic tension and resolution they add, how they increase in density (it can be played solo, by two pianists, four, six, etc.) and in the duration, which can be anywhere from forty minutes to several hours. It gets dense and powerful, like a train slowly building up speed, and then in the middle the textures settle to a steady consonance, and there is a luminous melody that is one of the most simple and beautiful in music.

#

The most important and famous minimalist composer outside of America, though, is the Estonian Arvo Pärt. The fascinating thing about Pärt's story is how he came to his unique, but truly minimalist, style independently of what was happening in America, and without hearing Reich's or Glass's music. In the years minimalism was growing something else was happening in Eastern Europe, behind the Iron Curtain during the decade or so before the fall of the Berlin Wall, that was quite similar to what had happened in Berkeley and San Francisco in the late 1950s and early 1960s. Composers who were dissatisfied with the status quo around them found a new path in personal spirituality allied with ideas from medieval music. But where La Monte Young was thinking in terms of medieval organum, and feeling in terms of Eastern philosophy and spirituality, Pärt was adapting organum through a very different technique, and feeling in terms of the Orthodox Catholicism prevalent in his home country of Estonia (he was raised Lutheran, which has a strong presence in Estonia, but later converted).

Pärt, whose public presence easily rivals Glass, if not exceeding it, is from the same generation as the original minimalists (he was born in 1935). He came to the method later in his career, not until the mid-1970s, but like the others he first tried his hand with serial technique. That had a much different context in the USSR. Creative culture was controlled by political power, and serialism was absolutely not orthodoxy and using it would place a composer under suspicion. It was temporary for him, as he was working through different compositional methods. Plainchant and the music of Renaissance composers like Josquin and Johannes Ockeghem refreshed his mind, and Orthodoxy refreshed his soul; both brought him to the style he calls "tintinnabulation." The word comes from the Latin for ringing bells, and it evokes his sound and what it gets at. Not that he uses bells, but that his music is full of moments where a chord or a bass note are let to ring and resonate with the space around them, like delicate, ringing bells, placed deliberately in space as in a ritual. His pace is moderate, even slow, his harmonies are basic triads—many times his pieces just spell out the harmonies in one direction, take a rest, spell them out in another direction, take another rest, and continue like that. It's what Glass does, but slower, lighter, quieter, internal. Glass's transition from the avant-garde to tradition goes through his practice of first exploring time in music, and then using his tools to express narrative and dramatic ideas in his operas and symphonies, while Pärt intriguingly uses the same means in order to get at something closer to La Monte Young's suspension of time. There's motion even as things seem to stay in place, a contemplative space that has made him possibly the most performed living composer of the twenty-first century, even though the style itself might be the most rigorously minimalist of any other composer.

His signature works *Fratres*, *Tabula Rasa*, and *Passio* use very little material and wield it with both extensive repeats and slight, significant changes that appear in some subsequent repetitions. Rather than a continuous flow of gradually changing music, he puts together different sections (though often only two or three) in a way also loosely similar to Glass. The sound of his work is both consonant and ascetic, it has the impersonal surface that Reich creates—though far more placid—but often has a specific liturgical story and if not, a powerful ceremonial feeling, there is a penumbra of mystery around it and a fundamental humanism.

He does do something special with repetition that, somehow, never disrupts the spiritual feeling of his music. Pieces like *Fratres* and *Tabula Rasa* are full of gripping intensity, at times dark and unsettling and cathartic in a ritualistic, non-narrative, manner. He doesn't proselytize, but his spirituality comes through as a somewhat irresistible force, a luminous presentation of his internal state. Pärt is the real thing, sincere, uninfluenced by the demands of the world around him. It may not convert anyone but it does capture the ears.

That's essential to his popularity, which is no mystery, there is a compelling beauty and the kind of timelessness and depth that is like drone music, but he achieves it through repetition. The effect is so strong that the producers of *Ted Lasso*[13] had one of the characters play his piece for violin, *Spiegel im Spiegel* in an incongruous moment in season three. The repetition and emotional weight of the piece nearly outshine the entire series. That repetition marks time in the way of classic minimalism,

---

[13] A sentimental sitcom on the Apple+ streaming platform about an American college football coach hired to manage a terrible British soccer team.

but somehow it doesn't feel like it. It's a remarkable body of work, and Pärt's craft, his ability to do so much with so little, is a profound contrast to the empty clichés of slow, gentle piano or cello lines recorded in rich ambience, full of inexpressive pauses, simplistic New Age music that gets labeled "minimal" and especially the generic and empty "modern composition."

Pärt is the answer to any question about both the reach and staying power of minimalism, its future legacy. Serialism has faded away as anything but a curious part of history, aleatory is part of the improvisation toolkit but Cage was such a singular genius that no one has been able to, or even been interested in, following his path. Then here's this quasi-holy man from the East, with exacting craft and serious purpose, who finds, that, yes, the way to make music about the spiritual mysteries of the infinite is to show the sound of the passing moments.

4 Post and Pop

Establishing the category of post-anything is like crossing the state line between Kansas and Nebraska; you've gone from one place to another, but did you even notice a change? It's all right in front of you but imaginary at the same time. There is a real and noticeable change though, the post-period of anything is more expansive, has more variety, touches on the borders of more ideas in related and parallel genres, all without necessarily being more diffuse. A new genre establishes tools, a post-genre explores their myriad uses. It's like a light cone diagram, which starts at a single point and the spreads out in all directions in space along one single direction in time. Minimalism is that point, the expanding cone is post-minimalism.

And expanding it is, even this moment as you read these words. Minimalism is a new standard in classical music, it is where the music has advanced in the mainstream tradit on for the past sixty years. It is, of course, one of many, as every idea and tool available out of the fracturing of the idea of classical composition after the Second World War is available to any composer who wants to use them. The classical composition landscape after the first quarter of the twenty-first century has no dominant style, and is so varied that it's impossible to say how many robust styles there are. This is made even more challenging because newly made music is still difficult to find in person and on recordings, so what does reach the ears cannot be considered fully representative. But some things are apparent: there is a strong Neo-Romantic movement of narrative expression, and a small subgroup in America of Black composers reviving the muscular, extroverted urban romanticism that was the main public alternative to serialism in the mid-twentieth century; many European composers make music that has an irreverent view toward both tonality and atonality, and an interest in setting up forms and fracturing them; the post-Cage Wandelweiser movement is strong and international in scope, making music that is in an indirect way an extended legacy of *Trio for Strings*, after it's been passed through more abstract but rigorous compositional forms, and made even quieter, more spacious, and far gentler; and there is post-minimalism, which just keeps heading down the road into the future, light on historical baggage but with an inherent knowledge that the tools of minimalism are the tools of history.

Where did this expansion start, and what are the qualities of post-minimalism? The minimalism that has been defined in this study means that post-minimalism is music composed with the fundamental quality of showing how music and time are intertwined and how they reveal each other, but that is no longer using that as the process of creating itself. Instead, it is a structural tool used to build forms that can have a more traditional teleology, that have a purpose toward which they are directed and at which they finish. If minimalism was a way to build a vocabulary of music in time—and it was—then post-minimalism is the new languages and dialects built with that. Minimalism cycled time from three hundred years of classical music and used it to make something new, now post-minimalism cycles time from the minimalist period (along with the history built into that) and plenty of contemporary music outside of the classical tradition to make something newer. The loops and grid of time continue.

The post-minimalist period didn't start with the musicians who came after Reich and Glass, but with the two themselves—and again with Meredith Monk ongoing developments. Peg it to Reich's *Music for Mallet Instruments, Voices and Organ*. In his conversation with Russell Hartenberger, they talk about that 1973 piece, one of the loveliest Reich has made, as the first time his music changed chords since 1965. Eight years without a chord change! Even in context, that's an incredible thing to consider for anyone making music in the West. "It felt great, it felt like liberation," Reich says, "It felt like 'oh, I can do this, too.' In other words, it's kind of one step forward for me, one step back in Western tradition."[1]

And there it is. Perhaps Reich is so good at articulating the details of minimalist music because he sticks to how it's made and how he would like to hear music move from one place in time to another, rather than what he's trying to say with it. By taking one step back into tradition, he's establishing minimalism as a practice that, from 1973, is part of the classical tradition and can be emulated by anyone, no matter their aesthetic goals. It is now a tool. The movement from minimalism to post-minimalism is demonstrated right there in his music, going from one ensemble piece that uses phasing, *Drumming*, through the non-phasing repetitive processing of *Music for Mallet Instruments, Voices and Organ*.[2] The experiment with making live music sound like a tape effect is over, now there's a new audible clarity to the method. There are also identifiable

[1] Steve Reich, *Conversations* (Toronto: Hanover Square Press, 2022), 66.
[2] This change in his music was documented in the important 1974 album that collected performances of *Drumming*, *Six Pianos*, and *Music for Mallet Instruments*, about which more in the next chapter.

sections rather than just a continual, gradual transformation from one state to another. You can count the number of repeats, you can count the number of notes being added or subtracted from a musical line, you can hear, like in the first vocal phrase in *Music for Mallet Instruments*, where the notes in the opening vocal and organ line are suddenly augmented while the mallet instruments below keep to the same number of articulated beats. The process is still laid bare, but it's different and far easier for other composers to adopt and musicians other than Reich's own to play. This all culminates in the masterpiece that is *Music for 18 Musicians*. It's a charming quirk of history that the piece that introduced minimalism to a general audience was one of the first post-minimalist works, and a daunting challenge to post-minimalist composers that they had to start by responding to that example.

All it took for this liberation for Reich—which opened the door for so many to follow—was the simplest idea in harmonic structure; use a second chord. Reich doesn't use harmony in the classical method, starting from home and building up tension through modulation before a satisfying return to home. He goes back again to Bach and the baroque, harmony is a thing to place the music in time, a pleasure to hear in itself. It seems to add color and variety as he began making more music that even had narrative and theatrical qualities. It's a sensible tool for vocal and choral works like *Tehillim* and *The Desert Music*, and quasi-documentary pieces like *The Cave*, *Different Trains*, and *City Life*, where Reich takes recorded speech, derives melodies and rhythms from it, then fits those into his repetitive structures. *City Life* even uses field recordings of traffic and construction noise as part of its rhythms and harmonies, in contemporary terms making Reich one of the early and most important adopters of sampling in classical music.

Placing chords in vertical slices implies both a hard edge to each beat and that things happen in sections, whether individual measures or groups of them. After *Music for 18 Musicians*, Reich uses episodic forms that are also bedrocks of history, the musical equivalents of chapters and paragraphs, and his most common large-scale method is to make pieces in three separate movements, almost invariably titled "Fast," "Slow," and "Fast." Utterly simple, utterly elegant.

Glass was working his way into post-minimalism at the same time. *Music for Mallet Instruments* is dated 1973, *Music for 18 Musicians* 1974–6. Inside that same period, 1971–4, was when Glass was working on *Music in Twelve Parts*. Though he uses harmony in a very different way from Reich, a horizontal flow of lines that's a masterful combination of both romantic era and Renaissance techniques, harmony was once again the single, enormous step. Pieces like *Music in Contrary Motion* and *Music with Changing Parts* had similar rudimentary harmonies to what Reich was using. Listened to in the order of their compositions, his works from 1968 up to *Music in Twelve Parts* seem to be pushing increasingly hard at just what kind of harmonies might appear as Glass added more horizontal instrumental lines to his repetitive loops. With lines running above and below each other, adding and subtracting notes, different combinations would meet each other, then depart and move on to the next. Nudged one slight step further, and you have voice leading, notes proceeding on independent lines designed so that they meet to establish satisfying harmonies, and follow through from one chord to the next. This is a basic compositional technique that Glass and every other classical composer learn. Minimalism for him, and also for Reich, seemed like a way to rediscover the value and utility of harmony.

Music in Twelve Parts completed that rediscovery, and as noted set down a comprehensive glossary of techniques and even phrases that Glass would use as the basics for everything that he has written through the proceeding fifty years. There are things as basic as the three-against-two rhythm (that can also be found in Brahms) that sticks deep in the mind from the very first listen to *Glassworks*. There are the harmonies and modulations between chords and keys in *Einstein on the Beach* that come directly out of the piece, there are the film scores and string quartets and further operas and symphonies, all with material that can be found in *Music in Twelve Parts* even as it may be thinned out or slowed down. It is also one of the great examples of how voice leading works and what can be done with it in classical music, and the other enormous doorway into post-minimalism. Reich showed how the vertical harmonies of the baroque and Stravinsky-ian modernism could be transformed by minimalism, Glass did the same with the enormous legacy of eighteenth and nineteenth centuries. The rest is post-minimalism, and post-minimalism is minimalism.

#

But what kind of minimalism is post-minimalism? The key word is still there because the process of explicitly working with time is still there, but it's different. As Kyle Gann wrote in *The Village Voice*, "It isn't watered down minimalism, Steve Reich minus the rigor." He notes that the tonality is still there, as are the basic rhythmic structures. Where Reich and Glass used those structures as also forms, showing and processing time, the post-minimalists used that, then went to another rhythmic structure, then another, and used a conventional scale or chord, then another, then another. Instead of a stream, they put different colored tiles in a row and that made their musical forms, like sections in a song. And those were both free and organic, fundamentally experimental, despite again not having the obvious difficult and complicated quality that has been the enduring, misleading signifier of both sophistication and innovation. Post-minimalism was and still is new, and that it is, like minimalism, often easy for the ears to grasp and appeals to listeners well beyond classical music doesn't show any lack of sophistication. Still, "Post-minimalism," Gann wrote, "may be the first avant-garde movement blasted by its opponents for a supposed conservatism."[3]

There's nothing inherently conservative about notes coming together in satisfying major and minor chords, or a beat and pulse that makes you want to tap your foot. Just as it's harder to write a good song than a good sonata, it's harder to make something that's both beautiful and interesting through repeated exposure than it is to make something that presents itself as difficult or obscure. Structural and sensual beauty and the skill and intelligence and taste it takes to create them are at the heights of artistic achievement, from Rembrandt to Ella Fitzgerald to Georges Balanchine. It is in the avant-garde in general and music in particular where modern culture has been trained to see beautiful things as conservative, and ugly things as breakthroughs—this even as American composer Lou Harrison was making stunning, beautiful, rich music in the 1950s and happily ignoring serialism. *Épater la bourgeoisie* is embedded in bourgeois artistic culture, and it feels like a great deal of the social condescension heaped on minimalism and post-minimalism has been because there is a self-consciously knowing viewpoint that doesn't think the music *épaters* the bourgeoisie hard enough. But add that to the notion that being

---

[3]   Kyle Gann, *Music Downtown: Writings from the Village Voice* (Berkeley: University of California Press, 2005), 247.

difficult and obscure was the measure of sophistication and artistic achievement, and you have a small and inherently conservative culture jealously guarding its dwindling status and relevance.

The actual music of post-minimalism, the life and variety in it as a field, is forward looking and creatively unsettled, always seeing where it can go next. It is progressive in both the sense of accumulating knowledge and in being and doing better. And there is a lot of it, a testament to how this is the living state of classical music. Gann, whose definition of minimalism is far more expansive than this study's, is a post-minimalist composer himself but not only that. He's made pieces with complex, computer-controlled cross-rhythms (*Nude Falling down an Escalator*), quiet, slow minimalism for three non-synchronized pianos (*Long Night*) and is an expert on microtonal systems. He published a discography of "Postminimal, Totalist, and Rare Minimalist Music" at his website that runs around 200 entries, and he apologizes for its "incompleteness."[4]

What it does indicate is that there's no one post-minimal style. The best tools are flexible and can be used off-brand. If minimalism is a useful, meaningful practice, then post-minimalism would show not just a variety of uses but some surprising ones. And that's exactly the case. Reich and Glass combined their present with ideas from the past, the post-minimalists did the same, and the present in places like New York City in the 1980s was appreciably different socially, politically, and technologically than San Francisco and Paris twenty years prior. Post-minimalists heard Reich and Glass, and also punk, disco, Afrobeat, and hip-hop, new materials and experiences to add to recent ideas. But the pull to express something with

4   https://www.kylegann.com/postminimaldisc.html.

music remained, so David Lang's *cheating, lying, stealing* uses minimalism in the way nineteenth-century composers would use sonata form as a means to an end, for him to express ideas about personal character, while Michael Gordon's *Yo Shakespeare* isn't about anything other than how to make, and play, ridiculously complex repetitive rhythms—and what those do to the listener.

Rock is an enormous part of post-minimalism, and would later make its way back to the minimalists themselves. That's just the process of music's progress repeated in our times. When in twelfth-century France, the hit song you work with is "L'Homme armée," when you're in New York City in the 1970s and 1980s, maybe it's Donna Summer, or something from Blondie or the Talking Heads. And you put it through the process.

These pages are a more restrictive fit than Gann's, as is the definition of the genre. There are worthwhile figures who just can't be included for the unfortunate reason that they were too obscure during their musical careers that they just weren't known beyond a circle of friends and cognoscenti. One example is Elodie Lauten (1950–2014), another is Julius Eastman (1940–90). Eastman's minimalism was both musically and political irreverent and also extremely focused and full of surprises. He had a brief career as an important vocalist, and was a member of Meredith Monk's ensemble. But drugs and mental and physical illness destroyed his life, and he died alone in a Buffalo hospital. Through the efforts of friends like the composer Mary Jane Leach, his music has been reconstructed and published, and it should be sought out; the combination of its humanity and the tragedy of his life is a powerful experience. But he was essentially unknown among his peers up to his death, and so it was impossible for them to feel his influence.

#

John Adams (born 1947) is the first name as he's one of the leading post-Copland/post-minimalist American composers. He's frequently included among the minimalists, but he never really was one other than some early, and very fine, pieces that explore the technique, like *China Gates* for piano and *Shaker Loops* for string orchestra. What Adams has done, though, that is immensely important, is that he took specific minimalist techniques of repetition and syncopation and combined them with expressive, Neo-Romantic ones, reconciling two separate parts of the classical tradition into something new that extended both into the future.

This has been a powerful combination. There's something inherently thrilling about Adams' sharp, nervous rhythms on the bottom and long lines on the top. He puts the allure of Reich together with the psychology of Gustav Mahler and the resonant harmonies of Jean Sibelius. His fantastic *Harmonielehre* (named after Schoenberg's harmony textbook) is one of the most performed contemporary symphonies, and his operas *Nixon in China* and *The Death of Klinghoffer* are superb and historically significant.

#

Tom Johnson (1939–2024): As noted before, Johnson was a composer as well as critic. He was an experimental post-minimalist, and his ideas of just how to work with and extended minimalism were quirky and ingenious. Before working with notes in time, Johnson worked with logic, and his minimalism is often an obsessive running through of the permutations of an idea—his gradual process is to run through conceptual iterations and see where they go. That means his *An Hour for Piano* is a handful of different textures for the instrument, played for an hour; *Rational Melodies* takes a simple melodic figure and edits and re-edits it through small, discrete, minimalist processes; *The Chord Catalogue* is exactly that, with a pianist playing "The 78 two-note chords," "The 1716 six-note chords," "The 78 eleven-note chords," etc. His incredible *Failing, a Very Difficult Piece for Solo String Bass*, takes logical thinking-through in a different direction. The solo bassist has to play the instrument while reading a text at the same time, which begins:

#

> In *Failing*, I am required to read a long text while playing music written above the text. The text must be read out loud at a more or less normal pace, and I must not allow the music to slow me down. The task is fairly easy for a while, because there is not much music, and most of it comes at the ends of clauses and sentences, almost like normal punctuation. Later on, there is more music, and the task becomes more difficult—so difficult, in fact, that I will probably not be able to do it without either slowing down my reading speed or else making mistakes in the music. At least the composer feels confident that I will eventually begin to run into trouble, which is why he called the piece *Failing*.

#

This does eventually become too difficult to play successfully, but that's the point of the piece, which is that the bassist is supposed to fail to play everything right, which means they have played it successfully. A perfect performance would be a failure.

#

Bang on a Can is not one composer, but three: Michael Gordon, David Lang, and Julia Wolfe. Bang on a Can is also a performing organization, with the Bang on a Can All-Stars quasi-house band, the Asphalt Orchestra new music marching band, a performance series, and the Cantaloupe record label. Heavily influenced by Glass and Reich, they are the premier post-minimal music establishment. They began the annual twenty-four-hour Bang on a Can Marathon concerts in 1987, where the only criterion was quality. Those put into practice the cross- and through-genre reach of minimalism. These were eventually pared down in the second decade of this century, but have returned as Long Play festivals centered on the Brooklyn Academy of Music the first weekend in May.

Those concerts recreate the Marathons. Each festival has been centered on the minimalism of Reich, Glass, Riley, and Monk, has also featured and honored the music of Captain Beefheart, Kim Gordon, Henry Threadgill, and Ornette Coleman, and of course the work of the three Bang on a Can composers. Like the generation that came before them, they've established the range and possibilities of post-minimalism. Gordon has composed some essential pieces, including *Yo Shakespeare* for a chamber rock ensemble of guitars and woodwinds playing complex, off-kilter, repetitive rhythms; *Industry*, which is gradual process music for solo cello played through a tube screamer amplifier; and the opera *Aquanetta*, about a B-horror movie actress and produced as if the audience is watching a film being made. Lang's *cheating, lying, stealing* takes process music and imagines it as expressive bad character, and his *Little Matchgirl Passion* has become a new staple of Christmastime concerts. Wolfe has written several pieces for vocalists and orchestra that portray some of the most fiery moments in labor history, like *Anthracite Fields* and *Steel Hammer*. Both Lang and Wolfe have won Pulitzer awards.

The All-Stars have recorded most of this music, and have also recorded *In C*, several of Glass's pieces, premiered Reich's *2x5*, and transcribed Brian Eno's *Music for Airports* album, turning it into a chamber piece that can be played by any ensemble, in concert. Call them an institution, they've earned it.

#

Mikel Rouse (born 1957): Rouse came to post-minimalism from Kansas City and his rock band Tirez Tirez. Not everyone would agree he's a classical composer, but he's a post-minimalist composer and his music shows how the practice of minimalism can work in rock, and that minimalism is a practice that works in many genres. He found ideas in Reich and African music, but for him the inspiration was the circular cross-rhythms of Afrobeat. He put this into practice with his Broken Consort, making post-minimalist chamber rock, but his metier has been multimedia operas that combine speech and song with themes from pop culture, including *Failing Kansas* about the Clutter murders immortalized by Truman Capote with *In Cold Blood*, and the astounding *Dennis Cleveland*, an opera in the form of a daytime television talk show.

#

Glenn Branca (1948–2018): Branca was the link between minimalism and experimental rock. He moved from playing in the No Wave band Theoretical Girls to making symphonies for large ensembles of electric guitars, enlisting peers like Thurston Moore, Lee Ranaldo, and Michael Gira. The massed, dense, repeated chords in his symphonies build up the sonic effect of a drone, one full of microtonal details. In the cycles of time, it's an unexpected result of the practice of minimalism, as if the repetitions open up a tear in the universe, and the listener looks in and sees the young La Monte Young.

#

Steve Martland (1954–2013): Martland was a British composer and one of Louis Andriessen's students. While Rouse and Branca came from rock and gathered in minimalist ideas,

Martland came from classical and wrote post-minimalist music with the punch and sound of a rock band. He used amplified instruments and complex progressive rock rhythms to produce exciting, brawny pieces, including his *Horses of Instruction* which was written for Bang on a Can. His *Patrol* for string quartet is closer to the sound of classical music, but still full of his exuberant attitudes about both sorrow and fun.

#

Cold Blue: Like Bang on a Can, not a composer, but an organization. Cold Blue is a label founded in the early 1980s that has been documenting a specific and identifiable California strain of post-minimalism. The label has its own sound, one that glows, but is not bright, sort of like the sun on a clear day in the Sierras, the warm disc in the sky while the air is cold and crisp. That's part of California minimalism, but the main part is an unexpected style that is built on minimalist repetition and gradual process music, but achieves some of the shamanistic and drone-like expressive qualities of Riley and Young. The central music on the label manages to use repetition to hold a still place in time, or a bubble where time moves differently inside from outside, a subtle and uncanny connection of Native wisdom and Einstein-ian physics. Cold Blue is a complement to Bang on a Can and doing just as much to further post-minimalism.

#

Minimalism hasn't just had a "post-" phase in classical music and its experimental edges, it's had an ongoing conversation and back-and-forth influence with pop music and with pop culture through non-musical media. To repeat, and repeat again: minimalism is a process first, a style second. That process is so useful, affecting, attractive, powerful as a technique and powerful in the minds and bodies of listeners, that it's been used across genres and styles. Minimalist composers didn't only appeal past classical music to pop but they showed musicians in popular music how music could be made in a certain way, and through playing and sampling they've taught invaluable lessons to two or three generations of musicians of all kinds who've followed them—and learned from those younger artists as well. Inside the rise of minimalism, everyone working on the music was learning how to make it, and from each other, as it went along. Pretty quickly those ideas started to make their way into the larger world, landing in some places that might have seemed surprising.

In his book *Repeating Ourselves: American Minimal Music as Cultural Practice*, Robert Fink points out features of American cultural experience from before the beginnings of minimalism to the mid-1970s, when the music was spreading out of its initial avant-garde niche and toward an audience larger than the one for classical music. Fink notes the popularity of LPs of baroque music and how, through advertising and marketing, they became a *de facto* ambient sound-bed in the home, the predictable and comforting structures of the music doubled in effect by automatic replay mechanisms; the spread of the Suzuki method of string instrument training from Japan to America in the late 1950s and early 1960s, herds of children playing the same patterns together, again and again, a combination of technical and ear training and discipline; the 1975 release of "Love to Love You Baby," sung by Donna Summer and produced by Giorgio Moroder and Pete Bellotte, with a nearly seventeen-minute extended album issue remix meant for long nights moving to mantra-like lyrics and hypnotic, repeated rhythms on the dance floor.

Did anyone grow up in mid-century America, hearing the baroque albums their parents put on the stereo, learning to play a little violin in Suzuki class during their elementary school years, then making their way to New York City (if not there already), dancing at Studio 54 after it opened in 1977? In one sense that doesn't matter, because "Love to Love You Baby," even in the extended version, had enough airplay that it hit the second spot on the *Billboard* Hot 100, and through the years its impact and influence has been honored by the Rock and Roll Hall of Fame, which named it as one of the "500 Songs that Shaped Rock and Roll," and VH1 put it on their list of "100 Greatest Dance Songs."

Two years later, Summer and Moroder and Bellotte released "I Feel Love," another hit (six on the *Billboard* chart) single that is one of the most incredible pop music songs ever recorded. Except for Summer's voice and the kick drum, the music is all synthesized, including the rest of the percussion, and laid out via sequencer. It reaches back and looks forward, with a pulse-based form and use of harmony and counterpoint that sets it as a striking middle ground between Reich and Glass. A shade past the disco of the era, it's closer to pure electronic minimalism and specifically Kraftwerk than it is to anything else. The inspiration of the sound of the song—an electronic music quality of it is the sheer force of it's colors and timbres, the rhythms are less important—launched The Human League and especially Blondie (one listen is all it takes to gauge this) as they became known, was rearranged by Beyoncé for her track "Summer Renaissance" on the 2022 *Renaissance*, and was elevated to the National Recording Registry at the Library of Congress in 2011. One measure of the importance of minimalism to all music genres is that there's an audible straight line from *Come Out* through *Music in Twelve Parts* through to "I Feel Love," and then out the other side to "Banteay Srey," a piece of slow-phasing gorgeous electronic minimalism on Carl Stone's superb 1991 album *Mom's*, released on New Albion.

Glass saw this, telling writer Kenny Berkowitz in 1997:

#

When I first heard Donna Summer, I just laughed. I said, "That's exactly what we're doing!" How could I miss it. And maybe it's a comment on the power of the ideas we turned up in this revolution. We came up with a few … techniques. It's like a tool … That's what we were doing in the'60s, we were inventing tools. And they turned out tc be very handy.[5]

#

Reich and Glass tossed those tools out into the world, and anyone could pick them up. Berkowitz notes that while in America, minimalism was hanging around in avant-garde spheres of music and art, in Europe the tools landed right on top of the world of pop. Kraftwerk, arguably the most important popular music band since the electric guitar was invented, clearly picked up the tools, which they used to expand their central style that began with *Autobahn* (1974).[6] The lineage of minimalism from them is even more stunning than that of Summer/Moroder/Bellotte; Kraftwerk is a foundation of early hip-hop, via Afrika Bambaataa, and techno through the innovations of Black musicians in Detroit. Elsewhere in Europe,

[5]   Kerry O'Brien and William Robin, eds., *On Minimalism* (Berkeley: University of California, 2023), 327. Originally from "Minimal Impact," *Option 77*, November–December, 1997.

[6]   A 2012 CD on Signum Classics, *Electric Counterpoint*, includes a percussion arrangement of the title piece by Reich and the Elysian String Quartet playing Kraftwerk's "Tour de France," "Radioactivity," and "Pocket Calculator," and they sound like siblings together.

Orbital and The Orb claimed Reich and Glass as inspirations— The Orb famously sampling Reich and Orbital making pale imitations of his tape pieces—although in the same article Berkowitz notes that the two composers shrugged aside the music of those producers, not hearing any connection or even much to interest them.

Back in America, Studio 54 (now a theater) was located in midtown Manhattan, about a dozen blocks from The Town Hall, where *Music in Twelve Parts* premiered June 1, 1974. That venue holds 1,500 people, not a huge audience on the global scale. But minimalism was already making its way onto records and therefore some airplay. Columbia recorded *In C* and released it in 1968 (*Rainbow in Curved Air* would follow in 1969 and then *Church of Anthrax*, the collaboration with John Cale, in 1971). Reich's electronic music had also been released by Columbia on their Odyssey imprint in 1967, part of a collection titled *New Sounds in Electronic Music*, and *Violin Phase* and *It's Gonna Rain* in 1968. By 1974, the flagship classical labels Angel and Deutsche Grammophon had issued *Four Organs* and *Drumming* (with *Music for Mallet Instruments, Voices and Organ* and *Six Pianos*), respectively. Some of Glass's rigorous experiments were out on his own small Chatham Square label, and 1976 saw the start of the first recording and releases of *Music in Twelve Parts* (initially in parts) on larger labels. The music was still a niche with the general public, but curious and in-the-know musicians could already hear some of the most important examples of minimalism in the mid-1970s.

That means while people were listening and dancing to Donna Summer, and going to see *Saturday Night Fever*, they could also hear Riley, Reich, and Glass. The albums and airplay were just picking up, but there were other chances to encounter the music. Making something new in the media age can have odd consequences. The Billboard rankings and the *American Top 40* weekly AM radio show mattered in pre-internet/pre-streaming radio environment. The bottom line was: how many records sold this week? The cliché about 1970s pop music and the album-oriented rock heyday of bands like Boston is that the music was bloated and dumb, but a look at the year-end Billboard rankings during the decade shows what anyone who grew up listening to the radio heard, which was that public taste was stylistically eclectic and broad. The top 100 singles for 1974 include Paul Anka's treacly "(You're) Having my Baby," Kool and the Gang's classic, almost wordless funk tune "Jungle Boogie," "Band on the Run" from Paul McCartney and Wings, Mike Oldfield's electronic prog-rock "Tubular Bells," Stevie Wonder, Jim Croce, Anne Murray, and more—the number one hit was Barbra Streisand singing the theme song to "The Way We Were." In 1978, when record buyers could pick up a copy of *Music for 18 Musicians* from ECM, listeners also bought Andy Gibb singing "I Just Want to Be Your Everything," "Hotel California" from the Eagles, Rose Royce doing the theme from "Car Wash," several hits from Fleetwood Mac's *Rumours*, and old school R&B/soul singer Joe Tex doing "Ain't Gonna Bump No More (With No Big Fat Woman)," coming in three places ahead of Captain & Tennille's "Muskrat Love." Neither of these were atypical years.

Public taste is not just one thing, and every bit of it is mysterious and mercurial (as well as being vulnerable to the effects of marketing) but it is not limited by ideology. There are subcultures beyond those of academic twentieth-century classical composers that insist music must fit into a set of rules, but the general public likes what it likes and historically has a broader palette than found in the subcultures (which exist mainly because the public palette is too broad). It's no surprise that the tool of minimalism, if not the music itself, would make its way into public listening via Donna Summer, Kraftwerk, and others. General listening has nothing to do with notions of how music should sound; it has to do with how it pleases the listener. So it's in the end not a surprise that it turned up in unexpected places for new music:

#

- In 1979, *Sesame Street* commissioned Philip Glass to make *Geometry of Circles*. This first aired on March 11, 1980, on Episode 1392 of the program. The music is a soundtrack for a short animated film that is something of a dance of six circles that rotate on top of each other and split to form kaleidoscopic patterns. This is an original work for chorus, keyboard, and percussion, not part of anything larger, and in the same style as both some of Glass's dance music and, with the voices repeating solfége syllables, the "Knee Play" music from *Einstein on the Beach*. Millions of impressionable young minds were hip to minimalism well before thousands of classical music administrators and label executives.

- In the early 1980s, at least one radio station, WXXI in Rochester, New York, used an excerpt of the bouncy flute solo from Steve Reich's *Octet/Eight Lines* (a later revision by Reich that kept the same flute part) as bumper music in between broadcast segments.

- On March 22, 1986, the Philip Glass Ensemble appeared on an episode of *Saturday Night Live*. They opened the show, rather than the studio band, playing an excerpt of "Facades," and then later played part of "Rubric," both from *Glassworks*. At one point during "Rubric" the image on the viewer's screen was replaced with a slow, time-lapsed pan of traffic flowing through Manhattan at night, a powerful and beautiful *Koyaanisqatsi*-like visual poetry rare on broadcast television. (Before it became just another brand, *SNL* was musically cutting edge and broadcast important avant-garde music to millions of American households, including The Clash, Gil Scott-Heron, Fear, Ornette Coleman, and Sun Ra.)

- September 9, 1986, Glass was the musical guest on *Late Night with David Letterman*. Letterman introduces him by saying he's one of the "few to successfully bridge the gap between classical and popular music," an unexpected bit of perceptive public musicology. Then Glass plays "Opening" from *Glassworks* solo on the piano, at a tempo about 50 percent faster than usually heard.

#

Glass especially is popular for producers and music supervisors on television shows and in movies. This does not count the sixty or so film scores he's written, including for *Candyman* (directed by Bernard Rose, 1992), *The Truman Show* (directed by Peter Weir, 1998), *Kundun* (directed by Martin Scorsese, 1997), and several of Errol Morris's documentaries—and then there is the Godfrey Reggio trilogy of *Koyaanisqatsi* (1982), *Powaqqatsi* (1988), and *Naqoyqatsi* (2002), multimedia creations that integrate film and music as a whole. More than any one thing, it is *Koyaanisqatsi* and its soundtrack that catapulted Glass to a new level of public recognition:

#

- Episode 10, Season 13, of the Fox animated comedy *Bob's Burgers* culminates in a xylophone ensemble playing the "Mishima / Closing" music from Glass's soundtrack to Paul Schrader's 1985 film *Mishima: A Life in Four Chapters*. It's one of the more magical moments in network television history. This soundtrack is so attractive in general that the "Mishima / Opening" music has also been dropped into the closing credits of an episode of the USA Network show *Mr. Robot* (Season 2, Episode 3).

- *Stranger Things* on Netflix re-popularized Kate Bush's "Running up That Hill" in Season 4, and that same season used the music from Act 1, Scene 3 of *Akhnaten*.

- The 1994 comedy movie *Camp Nowhere* (directed by Jonathan Prince) uses Reich's *Electric Counterpoint* in the soundtrack.

- Reich's *Variations for Winds, String and Keyboard* is part of the soundtrack for the 2021 film *The Humans* (directed by Stephen Karam), and it's in the company of "Knee Play 5" from *Einstein on the Beach* and Caroline Shaws third-generation minimalist *Valencia*.

- In what came as a surprise, Arvo Pärt's *Spiegel im Spiegel* has a prominent narrative role in *Ted Lasso*, Season 3, Episode 10, and also appears in Season 4, Episode 13 of the philosophical afterlife comedy *The Good Place*.

- The 2021 dance film *Birds of Paradise* (directed by Sarah Adina Smith) features Pärt's *Fratres*, putting the rhythmic minimalist bones of the music into prominence.

#

Glass has had a frequent enough presence on *The Simpsons* to almost qualify as a minor supporting character. That animated comedy is the finest chronicle of American popular culture since it premiered as a stand-alone show in late 1989. That matters because beyond just music, Glass appears as a cultural reference. Some examples are:

#

- In Episode 349, "The Seven-Beer Snitch," there's a scene in the Springfield Concert Hall, designed by Frank Gehry (who has a cameo). After the orchestra plays the opening statement from Beethoven's Fifth Symphony, the crowd gets up to leave, and Marge tries to stop them by standing in the aisle and saying, "Don't leave now, the next piece is an atonal medley by Philip Glass!" Now that's a multilayered joke.

- In Episode 159, "A Milhouse Divided," Homer tries to keep his marriage alive by buying tickets to shows at a theater Marge likes. He comes home and proudly shows her the shows: "Look, 'Mostly Madrigal.' Hey, that might be good. Oh, oh, 'An Evening With Philip Glass.' Just an evening?"

- Episode 456, "Stealing First Base," has a segment from an Itchy & Scratchy movie titled "Koyaanis-Scratchy: Death out of Balance," that uses time-lapse photography like *Koyaanisqatsi* and has music that's in Glass's style.

- Episode 436, "Eeny Teeny Maya, Moe," there's a commercial for the Prying Eye Surveillance nanny monitoring device shown on a TV ad, and the music uses a variation or Glass's film music.

#

While Reich hasn't had the same kind of broadcast television mass exposure and film scoring work that Glass has enjoyed, his music has been heavily sampled. Per the Who Sampled database (http://whosampled.com), he's been sampled almost sixty times. For popular music context, the database shows Fleetwood Mac has been sampled 198 times, Miles Davis 388, and James Brown 16,722, while recordings of Mozart have been sampled 268 times. The steady tempos and exacting rhythms of his music mean it fits easily into the quantization of digital audio workstations:

#

- A sample from *Come Out* introduces "America's Most Blunted" on *Madvillainy* from Madvillain (Stones Throw, 2004).

- "The Caliphate" from Earl Sweatshirt and The Alchemist album *Voire Dire* (Tan Cressida/ALC/Gala/Warner, 2023) also samples *Come Out* and interpolates it into the lyrics.

- Even if their music overall doesn't show much of Reich's or Glass's ideas, The Orb famously samples *Electric Counterpoint* for "Little Fluffy Clouds" on *Adventures beyond the Ultraworld* (UMG, 1991), probably their signature track.

- On his *Sakura* album (Lo 2000), Sakura samples *Music for 18 Musicians* and turns it into something close to a Reich remix on "Gekkoh."

- On David Bowie's *The Next Day Extra* EP (Jones/Tintoretto, 2013), there is an ingenious use of *Clapping Music* in the track "Love is Lost (Hello Steve Reich Remix by James Murphy for the DFA)."

- Deep house producer Kerri Chandler's "Six Pianos," on his EP *The Dark One, the Moon and the Candle Maker* (Deeply Rooted House, 2005), loops a sample from *Six Pianos* and then extends the sample through his own series of phases. There's also a 2017 EP on Kaoz Theory, also titled *Six Pianos*, with a new version and remixes from three other producers.

- Sukumu Yokota makes eerie use of a sample from Movement 1 of *Different Trains* for "Blood and Snow" on *The Boy and the Tree* (Lo, 2002).

#

There's also an entire album that Nonesuch produced in 1991, *Reich Remixed*, with various producers remixing tracks from his catalog on that label. There are re-workings of *Music for 18 Musicians*—chopped and sped up by Colccut—an atmospheric *City Life* made by DJ Spooky, and Ken Ishii turning *Come Out* into a tour-de-force piece of new electronica, complete with an audible beat.

Then there is the case of "Love on a Real Train" from Tangerine Dream's soundtrack to the 1983 Paul Brickman movie *Risky Business*. The movie was a hit, and this is one of Tangerine Dream's most popular single tracks. It has a compelling, gorgeous effect in the movie, and is enough of an imitation—though extremely well done—of *Music for 18 Musicians* that Reich contemplated suing the band. But it's not a straight copy, rather music made very close to the style of the original, and a generous listening can show it as a homage.

Getting in on the action himself, and adding layers of meaning and material to the expanding positive feedback loop that is the relationship between minimalism and popular music, Reich transcribes (not samples) Radiohead's "Everything In Its Right Place" and "Jigsaw Falling Into Place" into his 2014 piece *Radio Rewrite*, which along with *2x5* is his side of the ongoing conversation between contemporary classical composition and progressive rock that has been going on since *In the Court of the Crimson King*, from 1969. (Radiohead has been sampled 247 times.)

That second piece, *2x5*, is worth a further look. Reich composed it in 2008 for the Bang on a Can All-Starts chamber group. The All-Stars are close to a rock band. with an instrumentation that includes electric guitar and drum kit, and of course the Bang on a Can values of applying minimalist tools to quality music of any style, particularly rock. They're a bridge between minimalism and prog-rock, and Reich has had a notable influence on bands like Radiohead, King Crimson (the echt-Reich of the "Discipline" instrumental on their 1981 album *Discipline*), bits of Soft Machine and Sufjan Stevens, and the wonderful European band Akusmi, which is prog-rock in the style of Reich and Riley, or else minimalist chamber music played by a rock band, depending on where in the room you're sitting. Steve Martland would sit easily in a playlist with all these bands.

This is how musical influence works through history. Reich made music that musicians like Robert Fripp and Johnny Greenwood liked, and they wanted to make something using some of those ideas, and they did. Reich heard what they and others did, and with *2X5* wrote what is a piece of prog-rock chamber music. It utilizes pre-recorded tracks, as for *Different Trains*, to double the instruments, and the chunky guitar chords and bass riffs, the tricky drum patterns, are pretty straightforward prog. Influence is a continuing cycle, a flow of ideas from the past to the present, and even back into the past. Musical influence is the ongoing accumulation of cycles through time, like a Slinky that keeps on stretching farther while always being continuous.

The cherry on top of this is that along with releasing the *Double Sextet/2x5* album in 2010, Nonesuch the next year put out a three-track EP, *2x5 (Remixed)*, with three remixes of the piece from Dominique Leone, Vakula, and David Minnick. These put the rock back into the prog-rock minimalist chamber music that had put the minimalism into prog-rock, inside the ever-expanding universe.

Glass has been sampled even more, eighty-three times, including a few with the source label "The Philip Glass Ensemble." It's not clear if this says anything about the relative utility of their music for splicing into other tracks. Intuitively Reich's leaner textures and rhythmic emphasis would seem to fit more neatly into any sampling application or digital audio workstation, but Glass is a more prominent name, so …

#

- *Music Box* has been popular material, with samples from it in a wild range of music, including Travis Scott's "Days Before Rodeo: The Prayer" from *Days Before Rodeo* (Cactus Jack/Epic, 2014); the 2007 remix of Nelly Furtado's "Maneater" that features Lil Wayne; and Canibus's "Genabus" from his *Rip the Jacker* (Babygrande, 2003).

- The producer Aesop Rock grounds "Basic Cable," from *Float* (Rhymesayers Entertainment, 2012) with a sample from Glass and Shankar's *Offering.*

- Delorean cuts out and chops up a piece of Act 1, Scene 1: "Train" from *Einstein on the Beach* for the dance track "Real Love" (Subiza, Mushroom Pillow, 2010), with semantic hints of "Love on a Real Train."

- Glass's soundtrack music has been a popular sample source. K-Rino takes the opening credits music from *Candyman* for "The Phantom's Anthem" on *Alien Baby* (Black Book International, 2001).

- Shabazz Palaces uses "That Place" from the soundtrack to *Powaqqatsi* with a kind of maniacal focus on "The King's New Clothes Were Made by His Own Hands" from *Black Up* (Sub Pop, 2011).

- In six and a half minutes that poetically revive, expand, and honor the downtown New York City scene, Crabtree mixes together the gorgeous slow movement of Glass's Violin Concerto No. 1 with Debbie Harry's vocal track from "Heart of Glass," turning both into a powerful, haunting ballad (Suite 28, 2016). It is extraordinary and has been heard, in part, by millions as it underscores a protest scene in Season 1, Episode 3 of the Hulu series of Margaret Atwood's *The Handmaid's Tale*.

- Not sampling, but something else: Sia opens her "Breathe Me" (*Color the Small One*, Systemtactic/Go! Beat/Astralwerks, 2004) with a played transcription and interpolation of *Metamorphosis One*, writing a new song on top of specific ideas from Glass's piano piece, the old-school way that musicians hear music that speaks to them, take and modify elements and make something that's new and their own while showing the roots.

#

The idea of sampling dominates general thinking—because the market dominates thinking—about how musicians take music they like and rework it into their own stuff. But free from specific technology that is exactly how music has been made for thousands of years, even classical music. There is a common quote that appears in several versions attributed to multiple artists (Stravinsky, William Faulkner) but is one of those things that has the wisdom to be a truism: "Lesser artists borrow; great artists steal."

And like other great artists, and like Reich, Glass had his own relationship with music from others. Glass has written fourteen symphonies and is working on another; his First and Fourth used music and moods from two of the great collaborative David Bowie/Brian Eno albums, *Low* and *Heroes* (both RCA, 1977). In the continuing cycle of things, those albums were made by two artist who were also listening to Reich and Glass ("Weeping Wall" on *Low* is built on a bed very close to *Music for Mallets, Voices and Organ*). These are Glass's homages to Bowie, working themes from the albums into larger-scale symphonic writing, as he explained in a video conversation with Bowie taped in 1992—and the singer says he picked up the use of phonetics in his vocals from what Glass was doing at the time. At one point, Glass says, "People think about pop music or classical music as if these are fixed categories, but people that work in these fields … " and Bowie finishes the thought, saying, " … very rarely feel those confines." Glass also adds that composers who don't know what's going on outside of classical music are out of touch, and mentions that it's a collaboration across fifteen years, with Bowie's part done in 1977, and his in 1992 (for Symphony No. 1).[7]

This wasn't a weird blip or one-time thing for Glass. He and Kurt Munkacsi, the sound engineer for the Philip Glass Ensemble, produced two albums by the New York City band Polyrock. They formed in the late 1970s, after punk, and are new wave in the sense that they happened in that era, disbanding in 1983, but they're also quite something else. They have Glass's minimalist arpeggiations at the core, with a home demo "La Sol La Me" that could be the B-side of an *Einstein on the Beach* single, if there were such a thing. They chopped up Glass's flow into more angular rock chunks, have some of Talking Heads anxious energy, and even some bits of the B-52s. They are the first post-minimalist band, and if they're not quite prog-rock they absolutely anticipate math rock with tracks like "Bucket Rider." They put out two albums on RCA, *Polyrock* (1980) and *Changing Hearts* (1981), followed by a compilation of unreleased tracks a few years after they called it quits. Nor was Polyrock just a trivia answer; though it wasn't released until well after the fact in 2013 on Glass's Orange Mountain Music label, he and Munkacsi also produced an album by the solid

---

[7]   https://youtu.be/kb-5xktk_rU.

but generic new wave band The Raybeats in 1982. Philip Glass, unconfined, in touch.

That's how styles are created and mix and synthesize new things, continuing conversations through time. The accident of history means that Bowie and Glass could talk together about what they were doing, but Glass has those same conversations through his music with composers from long ago, as does Reich, as do the minimalists. Everything old isn't new again, everything new is made through ways that are as old as human culture. Those ways have given us so much to this point.

But there are still contemporary conversations to have. Glass had another with Richard D. James, aka Aphex Twin, who via Glass had his own conversations with Bowie and Eno. In 2003, Warp released *26 Mixes for Cash* and one of the tracks on that is "Heroes (Aphex Twin Remix)," a remix of both Glass's symphony and the original David Bowie track. But before that, in 1995, James asked Glass to add orchestration to one of his own tracks, and that became "Icct Cathedral (Philip Glass Orchestration)" on the EP *Donkey Rhubarb* on Warp.

To repeat, and repeat again: this is how music is made, and how the music called "classical" was made for close to 1,000 years, before the illusion that history had come to an end. It's no quirky thing, nor even "progressive" in the genre-scheme of things, for Pete Townsend to find inspiration in Terry Riley— The Who's "Baba O'Riley" (1971) is an out and out rock song, not prog-rock, and part of that is Riley himself was making music one small step away from popular styles. As were Reich and Glass, as was Mozart.

10 Essential Tracks

1. Terry Riley: *In C*
2. Steve Reich: *Drumming*
3. Philip Glass: *Music in Twelve Parts*, Part 1
4. Steve Reich: *Music for 18 Musicians*
5. Philip Glass: *Einstein on the Beach*, Act IV, Scene 3, "Spaceship"
6. Meredith Monk: "Gotham Lullaby"
7. Steve Reich: *Music for Mallet Instruments, Voices and Organ*
8. Meredith Monk: *Atlas*, Part 1, "Personal Climate: Choosing Companions"
9. Philip Glass: *Koyaanisqatsi*, "The Grid"
10. Simeon ten Holt: *Canto Ostinato*

Annotated Discography

Minimalism as music is inseparable from minimalism as discography. Like jazz, it's a new creation that quickly made its way outside small audiences in performance spaces to the general public. That was how it existed for all practical purposes for several decades, a music that existed on record albums, less often through the radio and the opportunity to attend a live performance. Little bits of it like *Geometry of Circles* and the flute solo from *Octet/Eight Lines* might unexpectedly appear and then just as quickly vanish, maybe teasing at someone's curiosity. But the way to hear more music like that was to find it on records.

That's modernist culture, creative work fully integrated with record-making and other documentation, recordings, and broadcast/streaming media as a replacement for concerts, music as an intriguing accompaniment to video. It's not a tautology to say that creative work that exists in large part because modern media exists is modernist; modern media makes it possible to establish new things that wouldn't exist without it. This is obvious with music videos, but because it began as a genuinely new and cutting-edge (if not avant-garde) music, the prime example is jazz. In 1917, the (all white) Original Dixieland Jass Band released "Livery Stable Blues" on a 78rpm disc. While not quite jazz as it would come to be, it was a way to hear a new style of music, and other musicians like Louis Armstrong and Bix Beiderbecke heard it and ended up making their own records, which spread the word to other musicians and listeners, etc. People learned jazz from records, and jazz developed as a music through musicians talking to each other and sharing ideas through the records they made.

Jazz is more a players' music, with improvisation the main thrust and musicians developing their styles through picking up ideas from others. Minimalism, as classical music, is more a composers' music. But other than *In C*, for more than a decade there were no minimalist scores that other composers could study and play. The reason that the early minimalist recordings, even the few for major record labels, are almost all played by the Philip Glass Ensemble and Steve Reich and Musicians is that beyond the fact these were the only groups playing this music, Glass and Reich were notating their music specifically for their musicians. And those musicians understood the non-standard language they were seeing, and working directly with Glass and Reich, while what the stuff looked like on paper would have been incomprehensible to anything from a classical chamber ensemble to a progressive rock group.

Discography is also where music collides with the market place and the business of record companies, where m stakes, chance, and short-sightedness are just as consequential as intention and effort. It's also a raw but useful metric for gauging a presence in the public, which expresses its taste and values with money. As music justifiably perceived as avant-garde by classical audiences and classical by people who listened to rock and jazz and the like, minimalism was never going to produce hit records, but it had enough commercial viability, and there were enough curious and eager listeners out there, so that it could endure as a recorded music until classical music and the general public caught up with it enough to incorporate it as a new mainstream in the classical tradition. Reich, Glass, and

Pärt are the main faces of classical music in the first quarter of the twenty-first century (Monk less so because classical music culture still has trouble with seeing her as part of it, even as she's composed for orchestras and string quartets, and fair enough; she uses the practice of minimalism in many not-quite-classical ways). And that's because their greatest works have been on records for fifty or more years.

Looking at the minimalist discography, then, is much more than just listing facts about recordings, it's a critical exploration of minimalism's relation with the listening public. The number of people who first heard, or mostly know, the music through albums like *Music for 18 Musicians* vastly outnumbers those who have been to a concert in a loft in SoHo, or even the cumulative total of audience numbers for every performance of *Einstein on the Beach* or *Music in Twelve Parts*. This stuff just does not get performed regularly outside of international cities like New York, London, and Tokyo, unless there's a city with a music school that has a new music ensemble that plays minimalist music once in a while. And the interplay between musicians/record companies/listening public has had at least one exceptionally important ramification, which is how the ECM label launched its New Series imprint with *Music for 18 Musicians*. That was certainly a gamble for Manfred Eicher, and it paid off well enough that the label started recording Meredith Monk in 1981, with *Dolmen Music*, followed by what is the main part of her career. Then in 1984, ECM released *Tabula Rasa*, unveiling Arvo Pärt and some of his greatest music to the West (and incidentally also introducing the great post-modern Russian composer Alfred Schnittke, who plays prepared piano on the title piece), and now Pärt is possibly the most performed living composer of this century. As the years go on, it's becoming increasingly clear that what ECM is at its heart is less a jazz label than the most important source for the expanding post-Second World War Western classical music tradition.

The discography also preserves the history of minimalism in critical ways. More than just following dates and hearing how things developed, it's the way to hear certain pieces that may have only a few years left for public performance. This is specifically the case with Philip Glass Ensemble works. While he has a huge amount of music written for standard classical ensembles and instrumentation that anyone can pick up and play, the most important works originally for the Ensemble are still only played by that group. *Music in Twelve Parts* is the most piquant example. This is still a specialized piece and demanding to play. Glass himself has stepped away from the keyboard for it, and while his long-time music director Michael Riesman still plays and leads the Ensemble, the fiftieth anniversary concert at Town Hall in 2024 appeared to show he has limited time left with this music, as there were some crucial mistakes that came close to causing total disaster. The Ensemble has handled changes through the years, with the current wind players and the soprano replacing the original members, and Mick Rossi now on Glass's former keyboard part, but it's an open question whether they can continue after Riesman has stopped playing. But as long as one can press play on a recording of that, or any minimalist music, the sound waves will vibrate and the music will live.

#

Drumming/Music for Mallet Instruments, Voices and Organ/Six Pianos (Deutsche Grammophon, 1974): This is the 3-LP box set that turned out to be so consequential to Reich's career and overall discographical history. It is still an excellent recording of this piece—there's no bad recordings of *Drumming* and everything that Steve Reich and Musicians put down on tape is the reference for every other recording. Since the initial release, this has been repackaged on two CDs several times, and is of course available digitally. As important as the document is, Deutsche Grammophon has been appallingly lazy with each CD/digital reissue: due to the duration limits of 33 rpm LPs, the original pressings had to take music that seamlessly moves from one section to the next and fade out at the end of one side and in at the start of the next. And yet, even the most current digital version fades out at the end of Part 3 and in at the start of Part 4. Listening-wise, this is a minor irritation, in a larger context it reveals how the record business is just a business, and even labels that have the façade of being dedicated to preserving and spreading great music don't really care all that much. That being said, this is a cornerstone recording to have as it also includes *Six* Pianos and the utterly gorgeous, post-minimalist *Music for Mallet Instruments, Voices and Organ*.

The first recording of *Drumming* came out in 1972 from the John Gibson + Multiples imprint. This is the only release, ever, on that label and was a private edition with limited distribution. In 2018, Superior Viaduct reissued it on CD and LP. This is a recording made at Town Hall in December 1971, when the music was still brand new and getting its first performances. While this had too few listeners to be historically important, it is the single best available recording of the piece, with the palpable tension of musicians diving into something that produced some anxiety along with excitement. Not necessary, but something every Reich fan will want, it is unfortunately out of print and not available digitally, but copies can be found for reasonable prices on the secondary/used market. And while Superior Viaduct does not sell a digital version, they do have important digital reissues of early minimalist and post-minimalist music from Jon Gibson and Tony Conrad.

For non-Reich helmed recordings, the Colin Currie Group and Synergy Vocals—effectively part of the Steve Reich and Musicians for decades—released their own recording of *Drumming* in 2018, and this is one of the very best versions. The playing is not just fantastic but fast[1] and intense, even in the quiet chiming that opens Part 3. The French new music group Ensemble Links, which is making *Music for 18 Musicians* into their specialty (more on that below), has a streaming-only recording which is the most recent. It's exceptional, and Reich himself has praised it: "The tempo is fast, the playing is light and crystal clear and the recording is beautifully balanced. The blend of voices and marimbas is pure magic. Bravo!"[2]

While there are, again, no bad recording of this, there is a curious one that may or may not please listeners. The Japanese percussionist Kuniko has an ongoing project to play Reich's ensemble music solo, prerecording tracks and then playing live along with them, moving from part to part and instrument to instrument in the manner that Reich himself devised for the solo flute piece *Vermont Counterpoint* and then used in *Electric* Counterpoint, *Different Trains*, *Triple Quartet*, and others. Her playing is impressive, but there's certainly something lost without the drama and humanity of a bunch of musicians working together. Caveat Auditor.

[1]   An interesting feature of recordings of *Drumming* is that through the years they've gotten faster, as if the musician have gotten better at playing the music.
[2]   https://www.ensemblelinks.fr/recordings.

Music for 18 Musicians (ECM, 1978): Another reminder that the music business is just a business is the fate of the Deutsche Grammophon recording of *Drumming* and the ECM release of *Music for 18 Musicians*. The studio recording on this album was actually made by Deutsche Grammophon, but was never released to the public, only getting a promotional pressing on LP. Apparently, the company was disappointed in the sales of *Drumming* and gave up on the new recording and Reich. Their loss was ECM head Manfred Eicher's gain, and in a sense history's and ours as well. With Beryl Korot's abstract patterned image on the cover, this is the recording that introduced Reich to a larger audience, eventually hitting six figures in sales, and also launched the "New Series" imprint on ECM which in retrospect has more clearly defined that label and its place in discographical culture than their jazz releases. The cultural impact of this album is that it is *the* music people think of when they think of Reich, was the rare new music album that got reviewed in *Rolling Stone* (by John Rockwell for the April 18, 1979 issue), and was named by David Bowie as one of his favorite albums in the November 2003 issue of *Vanity Fair*:

> Bought in New York. Balinese gamelan music cross-dressing as Minimalism. Saw this performed live in downtown New York in the late 70s. All white shirts and black trousers. Having just finished a tour in white shirt and black trousers, I immediately recognized Reich's huge talent and great taste. The music (and the gymnastics involved in executing Reich's tag-team approach to shift work) floored me. Astonishing.

Reich wrote this and other pieces of the time for his ensemble, so used a shorthand notation that he and the musicians understood—there was no generally available score, so nothing for another group to pick up and start playing.[3] But the effect of the music was so powerful that eventually the German group Ensemble Modern constructed their own score by listening to and transcribing the two versions available at the time (the ECM release and a new recording made for the Nonesuch collection *Steve Reich: Works 1965–1995*). They recorded this for RCA/BMG and released the CD in 1998, and that unlocked the floodgates. One result was that Reich's publisher, Boosey & Hawkes, compiled the piece into a score that any ensemble could play.

It can't be overstated how important this is. The repertoire of classical music exists not only because people love to play and hear it, but because it's available via scores, the information and instructions preserved and spread on paper. That's how music that was a specialist matter at the time, played by musicians in close collaboration with the composers and often notated in a way only understood by this small group, begins to spread into both public consciousness and history. That's how a niche becomes a common practice and a legacy.

As of this writing, there are ten different recordings in the discography, only two by Steve Reich and Musicians. The recommended ones are:

- Amadinda Percussion Group, *Music for 18 Musicians Live in Budapest* (Hungaraton Classic, 2004): This one is a little subdued at first, but rises to greater intensity and excitement than any other version.

[3] There's an interesting exception in a 1984 EMI album from i Solisti New York, conducted by flutist Ransom Wilson, where the ensemble plays Reich's *Eight Lines* paired with John Adams's *Grand Pianola Music*. Later CD reissue included Ransom's recording of the multitrack solo flute piece, *Vermont Counterpoint*.

- Grand Valley State University New Music Ensemble, *Music for 18 Musicians* (Innova, 2007): Bill Ryan, a teacher at GVSU in Michigan and director of the ensemble, put this project to the young musicians, and they produced this tremendous, powerful, moving recording.

- Ensemble Links, Rémi Durupt, *Music for 18 Musicians* (Kairos, 2020): There are some disconcerting inflections from the European vocalists on this recording, but otherwise this makes the case for being the single best performance, with a sense of eager fun, an urgent pressing-forward feeling and real power.

- Colin Currie Group, Synergy Vocals, *Music for 18 Musicians* (Colin Currie Records, 2023): UK percussionist Currie has taken up the torch of Reich's great early works, all his concerts and recordings of the music are recommended. This one opens up a near-spiritual sensation.

There are also recordings to avoid. There are one-man band releases, put together via solo musicians using multitracking and overdubs. While the techniques and dedication are impressive, the listening experience is terrible. Reich is a composer, he writes music for people to play together. Making music is a social activity, and even if you can't see it, the way musicians have to work together in his music has an expressive power all on its own—you can hear what Bowie saw. That is essential to the experience of his music, and solo recordings have none of it.

Back to the significance of *Music for 18 Musicians* becoming part of the classical repertoire so that any interested group can play it; this is first of all such a brilliant work that any group of musicians up to the specialized physical, and especially mental, demands of tackling it are going to produce a beautiful performance. It's a special work that way; the process of the music is so fundamentally simple and powerful that it almost plays the musicians, not the other way round. That means remarkably, there are different interpretations. While there're some choices the musicians can make about repeats, the details are mostly plain, and the things that musicians and ensembles normally use to show their own expressive choices, especially changes in dynamics and tempos, simply aren't there. There's only one way to play it.

Except the more groups that play it, the more they can play it differently in subtle but noticeable and meaningful ways. Each performance has its own mood because the musicians and audience are mostly different each time. But that's a subtle thing, hard to discern and define. Each performance can also have a different style, and there's an example of this on YouTube. There are two full, live performances of this piece, one played by Ensemble Signal at Jazz at Lincoln Center in July 2016,[4] the other by Bang on a Can, augmented by a dozen or so musicians, for the Long Play festival at the Brooklyn Academy of Music, May of 2024.[5] Both are among the best new music groups, Ensemble Signal is part of the core of overall new music performance, and many talented, highly trained young musicians pass through its rank, while Bang on a Can is the veteran performing group of the central post-minimalist movement. Roughly, Signal is more "classical" while BoaC is at the edge, and crosses over, into jazz and progressive rock composition. Signal's performance is beautiful, with a refined, rich balance between all the instruments that produces a

---

[4]   https://www.youtube.com/watch?v=BXVjf_
      FSqpc&list=WL&index=26.
[5]   https://www.youtube.com/watch?v=kKO3lcvdWUQ.

kind of velvet purple sound, and there's a smoothness to their rhythms and how they shape the notes that's just gorgeous. They also change the weight slightly on the musical phrases in the final sections so they sound different from any recording, while still being exactly the same piece. BoaC, meanwhile, has more dance-like energy, a little rougher around the edges, a little sharper in all the notes, a little more force, a little more rock. It's an extremely good thing for the music when it hits a critical point where not only are multiple ensembles playing it, but they're finding ways to play it their way.

#

Different Trains/Electric Counterpoint (Elektra Nonesuch, 1989): Along with the music above, this is the remaining essential pillar in Reich's discography. The main point here is the blunt, abrading narrative about the Holocaust, with the metaphor of trains as both wonderful transportation (he took them from New York to Los Angeles regularly as a child to travel between his divorced parents) and the means to haul Jews to the death camps. There are recorded reminisces from Pullman porters and Holocaust survivors, and Reich used the shape and cadence of those to make his melodic lines and rhythms. Full of physical energy and emotional power, it's a masterpiece, made for the Kronos Quartet which plays it here. (The album also has guitarist Pat Metheny playing the delightful, sample-inspiring *Electric Counterpoint* for solo guitar and backing tapes. This might be Reich's most recorded piece, it just takes a skilled and enterprising electric guitarist. With that, it's also open to a wide range of interpretation, depending on the sound of the guitarist. Metheny plays with his bright, clean articulation, the air seems to shimmer. Radiohead guitarist Johnny Greenwood plays it on the same album with *2x5* and it's full of grit and a crunchy rock sound.)

Made in the form of a regular, notated and published score, there are several other recordings of this, and for anyone looking to augment the original, the best choices are from the Smith Quartet—*Different Trains* (Signum Classics, 2005)—and the Mivos Quartet's 2023 release of Reich's complete *The String Quartets*, which includes *WTC 9/11* and *Triple Quartet*, ironically on Deutsche Grammophon. Some businesses can learn.

#

There is also a one-stop, complete, doorstop box issued by Nonesuch in March, 2025, *Steve Reich: Collected Works*. This is indeed all his notable music, from *Come Out* to *Jacob's Ladder*, which premiered at the New York Philharmonic in the Fall of 2023 and was first issued as an album as both part of this box and separately. There is at least one more unrecorded Reich piece, *Two Pianos*, composed in 2020 and set for premiere at Town Hall as part of a 2024 concert that was cancelled. Presumably it will be heard someday. Note that this box includes both the recording of *Music for 18 Musicians* that had been made for the previous Nonesuch collection and also a fine one from Ensemble Signal and conductor Brad Lubman, originally released in 2015 on Harmonia Mundi, and as with that piece Nonesuch made a new recording of *Drumming* as part of their previous Reich collection.

#

Philip Glass Ensemble, *Music in Twelve Parts* (Venture 1988/Virgin 1990); Philip Glass Ensemble, *Music in Twelve Parts* (Nonesuch, 1996); Philip Glass Ensemble, *Music in Twelve Parts* (Orange Mountain Music, 2007); Philip Glass Ensemble, *Music in Twelve Parts: Concert a Paris* (partial recording) (Transversales Disques, 2019): This magnum opus has an interesting discographical history. That a four-hour work that can only be played by a specialized ensemble gets any recording is not to be taken for granted, and that the recording process for this piece began relatively soon after its 1974 premiere indicates Glass's burgeoning stature in the mid-1970s. Caroline/Virgin released an LP and cassette of the first two parts in 1976, while the first recording of the full work was a multi-year process that began in May 1975 with the first half. The remaining six parts were put down in 1987, with the entire work released on vinyl and cassette in 1988, then CD in 1990.

With a dozen years in between the two sessions, this release (now out of print but easy to find on the used market) tracks changes in the Philip Glass Ensemble. Saxophonist Dicky Landry is in the group for the first session, later replaced by Jack Kripl, the same for sopranos Joan La Barbera and Dora Ohrenstein. The Ensemble also plays the music in slightly different ways between the two halves, and there's the fascinating quality of hearing their early interpretation and the manner the group took on after playing the music for years. The first half is very different from the second, and very different from the two later complete recordings, it's more relaxed, transparent, there's different emphases on the rhythms and the phrases, and even slight differences in the composition itself. In the intervening years Glass added or changed notes here and there and structured some rhythms differently, sort of pushing them just a bit in one direction of another. The second half points toward the Nonesuch and Orange Mountain releases, which are generally faster, and have a little more swing and intensity to the playing.

Of the three, then, the latter two are quite similar in how the group plays the music, the main difference is in the timings of the different sections. The Venture/Virgin recording is starkly different. All of them are excellent, gorgeous, and powerful, but there's a specialness to the first of them, a delicacy and charm that are beguiling, plus Sol Lewitt designed the album cover (a Frank Stella painting adorns the cover of the Orange Mountain set). That's also true for the Transversales Disques 2-LP release. These are live on French radio recordings of the ensemble playing Parts 1, 2, 3, 11, and 12 in 1975. The feeling is also relaxed here, at times even careful, like the musicians are still working on completely incorporating the music into their minds and muscles, and there are a few (inconsequential) mistakes. The historical significance will appeal to Glass fans, as will side D, which is an interview with Glass in his rehearsal studio in 1974, while they're working on the piece that was produced by French radio and is conducting entirely in French, by both the interviewer and Glass. Know your languages!

#

Philip Glass Ensemble, *Einstein on the Beach* (Tomato/CBS Masterworks, 1979); Philip Glass Ensemble, *Einstein on the Beach* (Elektra Nonesuch, 1993): Like *Music in Twelve Parts*, it's rather amazing that this deeply avant-garde five-hour opera was ever recorded, and there are two excellent recordings! The first was released on the independent Tomato label with distribution by CBS Masterworks (the CD reissues have been on CBS and later Sony, when they bought CBS). The draw here is the original cast, most prominently actor Samuel M. Johnson. He wrote the soliloquies for his role, and his idiosyncratic elegance and charisma in the speaking parts are unforgettable. Paul Zukofsky, a superb and important new music violinist, plays the "Knee Plays," and Robert Palmer contributed to the liner notes.

Again, the ensemble personnel changed in the intervening years, and the bottom line is that the group did get a little better. The instrumental playing on the Nonesuch recording is slightly, but noticeably, superior, as is the sound of the recording, which is deeper and richer. Zukofsky has been replaced by the equally fine Gregory Fulkerson, Lucinda Childs is back to say "These are the days my friends." The major difference is that Jasper McGruder has replaced Johnson in the acting role. He's quite fine, but Johnson was unique. The choice is between yin and yang, the first recording has non-musical history with it, but the second is a slightly better album.

#

Glass has been a prolific composer and his discography (both in and out of print), is enormous, and along with the recordings of certain pieces, there are re-recordings with different instrumental variations and arrangements. Being a more traditionally classical composer means that many soloists and small ensembles have played and recorded his music. His Etudes alone, which were published in full in 2012 and are now a core part of the entire classical piano repertoire, have been recorded in full or part over two dozen times. There have also been several fine collections issued, each with variety and depth, but those are unfortunately out of print (they can be found used), though it's likely that the labels that have substantial parts of his back catalog, specifically Nonesuch and Sony, will repackage/reissue their holdings in the not distant future (Since 2001, Glass has released new and back catalog recordings on his own Orange Mountain Music label). Here are selected recordings that outline the range of his music and also cover more of his greatest pieces:

#

- *Alter Ego Performs Philip Glass* (Orange Mountain Music): A generous set with early pieces *Music in Similar Motion*, *Strung Out*, *Piece in the Shape of a Square*, *Gradus*, *Music in Contrary Motion*, *600 Lines*, and *How Now*.

- *Kronos Quartet Performs Philip Glass* (Nonesuch): Superb performances of String Quartets Nos. 5, 4 "Buczak," 2 "Company," and 3 "Mishima."

- Vikingur Ólafsson, *Philip Glass: Piano Works* (Deutsche Grammophon): This has "Opening" from *Glassworks* and about half of Glass's Etudes. Ólafsson is a tremendous pianist and there is more weight of meaning in his playing than anyone else.

- Anton Batagov, *Philip Glass: The Complete Piano Etudes Live in Moscow* (Orange Mountain Music): There are many recordings of the Etudes, and many good ones. This is the best single collection, if you can only have one single collection (Glass plays them too, and they have a great feel but he's not the pianist Batagov is).

- Philip Glass Ensemble, *Glassworks* (CBS): A Glass classic. *Glassworks* is usually played on the piano, but it's best in the full orchestration for ensemble.

- Dennis Russell Davies; Sinfonieorchester Basel; Stuttgart Chamber Orchestra; Vienna Radio Symphony Orchestra, *Philip Glass: The Symphonies* (Orange Mountain Music): There are a small handful of recordings of Glass's first three symphonies, but this is the only collection so far. These are uneven pieces, and the way Glass reuses his material doesn't always fill out some of these pieces. But this is still his first ten symphonies. His more recent Nos. 11–14 (Symphony No. 12 is based on the Bowie album *The Lodger*) have been excellent, hopefully this collection will be updated. In the meantime, Orange Mountain has released digital recordings of the later symphonies, including the masterful Symphony No. 11.

- Soundtracks: the essential one is for *Koyaanisqatsi* (Nonesuch), and highlights of the rest include *Mishima* (Nonesuch), *Dracula* (Nonesuch), and *The Music of Candyman* (Orange Mountain Music).

#

There is one more recording to flag, not because it's a best-of, but because it's so unusual. In 1994, Glass composed music for the Cocteau film *La Belle et la Bête*. But this is not a soundtrack, instead it's a hybrid film score and opera. Glass took the dialogue from the film, set it to music, and synced it to the movie. It's performed as an ensemble piece with singers while the film rolls. This doesn't completely work, as forcing the dialogue in real time into the music makes for some awkward vocal passages, but it's ambitious and the high points are poetic and lovely. There's a recording of this on Nonesuch.

#

Meredith Monk has mostly recorded for ECM, and in 2022 the label released a collection of all their albums of hers, *The Recordings*. It is everything, from *Dolmen Music* to *On Behalf of Nature*, and includes *Atlas*. This speaks for itself, and is valuable because many of these single albums are out of print. While a small handful of musicians, like pianist Bruce Brubaker, play some of her pieces, her work is still mainly in the situation Reich and Glass had, of requiring her own specialist vocal/instrumental ensemble.

For single recordings, *Atlas* is of course a must, there's nothing like it. Of the rest, *Dolmen Music* is one of the best representations of her work, as is *Do You Be*. In 2009, John Zorn's Tzadik label released *Beginnings*, a wonderful collection of early Monk. She plays the guitar and sings a crystalline "Greensleaves," experiments with a duo for voice and Echoplex, and sings early versions of "Biography" and "Do You Be?" Many of these tapes are live, and they show her working up to "Gotham Lullaby" and more.

#

Terry Riley, *In C* (Columbia Masterworks): Since *In C* is available to anyone who can download the score, there are a lot of performances and recordings, but the first one should always be the first one. This is a discographical landmark for minimalism and avant-garde music, a reminder that sometimes amazing things happen in big corporations (in this case because Columbia had hired computer music composer David Behrman and let him produce a contemporary music series), and on top of that Riley leads the ensemble and plays the saxophone—and Jon Hassell plays trumpet.

Louth Contemporary Music Society, *Terry Riley: IN C Irish* (Louth Contemporary Music Society): One of the most recent recordings comes from this Irish new music organization. This is a live album, with traditional instruments like the Irish harp and uilleann pipes. It has amazing spirit and energy and is one of the best.

#

Edo de Waart, San Francisco Symphony, *John Adams: Harmonielehre* (Nonesuch): Adams's music, especially this great symphony, is a shining example of what post-minimalism can be. He uses repetition and the process of shifting rhythms through variations as a tool combined with ideas that reach back to Stravinsky, Mahler, and other titans of the classical tradition. A key rosetta stone in classical music history, from the crashing, repeated E minor chords at the start to the end, it's a gripping listen. One of the most often played modern symphonies, there are many recordings, and several good ones, but this first one, from the first orchestra to play it, has an exciting edge.

John Adams, London Sinfonietta, *John Adams: Chamber Symphony / Grand Pianola Music* (Elektra Nonesuch): Adams has a narrative streak in his music, he's upfront about his desire to tell audiences things—that's the traditional expression conveyed with some minimalist procedures. But his best music can often be about nothing, and that's *Grand Pianola Music*. This is post-minimalism that's full of fun and wit, tenderness, and elation, all through musical gestures. *Chamber Symphony* is Adams's own version of both cartoon music and Schoenberg.

#

Gidon Kremer/Keith Jarrett; Dennis Russell Davies/ Staatsorchester Stuttgart; The 12 Cellists of the Berlin Philharmonic Orchestra; Gidon Kremer/Tatjana Grindenko, Alfred Schnittke, Saulus Sondeckis, Lithuanian Chamber Orchestra, *Arvo Pärt: Tabula Rasa* (ECM): This is one of the great albums of minimalism and one of the key new music recordings of the twentieth century, as valuable as *Music for 18 Musicians*. Pärt's composing is simple and graceful and also granitic, so each repeated phrase and idea gradually builds weight and intensity. Violinist Kremer and jazz pianist Jarrett play beautifully, and the side B performance of *Tabula Rasa* is haunting and has never been bettered.

#

Simeon ten Holt, *Canto Ostinato*: Dutch pianist Jerome van Veen has made a specialty of this masterpiece of minimalism, a work that's on the same level as the most important music from the American founders of the movement. This is usually played on the piano—it's a chordal, polyphonic piece—but doesn't have to be. Van Veen has recorded multiple versions; solo, for two and four pianos, for three pianos and organ, for two pianos and two marimbas, for two prepared pianos, for synthesizers, etc. These also vary in duration from about seventy minutes to two and a half hours (there is also a release, *Canto Ostinato XXL*, with organ and two piano duos that fills over four hours). These recordings are released on CD, LP, and digitally on the Brilliant Classics label and are available individually and in an *XL* collection of multiple versions. Like *Drumming*, there are no bad versions of this piece, but the very best are the ones for four pianos and for three pianos and organ.[6]

#

Bang on a Can has a few collections with some real post-minimalist classics. *Live Volume 1* (CRI), direct from a Marathon, opens with Tom Johnson's *Failing*, and includes Julia Wolfe's *The Vermeer Room*. *Industry* (Sony) is titled after Michael Gordon's piece of screaming minimalism, has Wolfe's *Lick*, David Lang's percussion classic *The Anvil Chorus*, and Louis Andriessen's gnarly *Hout* and *Hoketus*, in which he takes a medieval rhythmic structure and turns it into twisty post-minimalism. *Cheating, Lying, Stealing* (Sony) has Lang's classic, and the album was reissued by Cantaloupe as *Classics*, this time including Gordon's *Industry*.

#

Ransom Wilson and i Solisti New York, *John Adams: Grand Pianola Music; Steve Reich: Eight Lines/Vermont Counterpoint* (EMI, 1985); Ransom Wilson is a flutist and conductor, and he leads the i Solisti chamber orchestra and, as a solo flutist, plays Reich's *Vermont Counterpoint*. This is a soloist/tape piece that

---

[6] For the curious, van Veen has also recorded Satie's minimalist-adjacent *Vexations*, on Brilliant Classics, playing all 840 repeats in one session, a complete and continuous recording that lasts nearly twenty-four hours and is quite an experience.

predates *Electric Counterpoint* and has the same bouncing, shimmering counterpoint, with the flutist moving between a regular instrument, bass flute, and piccolo. The pairing with Reich's and Adams's chamber pieces is a good one, this is a fine alternative to the recording of *Grand Pianola Music* that John Adams conducts.

#

London Chamber Orchestra, *Minimalist* (Virgin Classics, 1990): This is an ideal collection of minimalist and post-minimalist music, and a fine example of how minimalism started moving into the repertoire for standard classical music ensembles. This has *Shaker Loops* from John Adams, Reich's *Eight Lines*, *The Frontier* from English composer David Heath, and two from Glass: *Façades*, with gorgeous saxophone solos by John Harle and Simon Haram; and *Company*.

#

Icebreaker, *Terminal Velocity* (Argo, 1994): One of the essential albums of post-minimalism, this CD was the first chance many had to hear Michael Gordon's *Yo Shakespeare*. Icebreaker is another post-minimalist rock style ensemble, dense with guitars, and on this album they also play music from Andriessen, Gavin Bryars (the languid, minimal *The Archangel Trip*), Damian le Gassick, and wrap it up with an unclassifiable piece by David Lang, *Slow Movement*. That sounds like a rough, heavy, dirty stone, full of fascinating flaws, pockmarks, and chinks, slowly turning in space.

#

Michael Tilson Thomas, Ralph Grierson, Roger Kellaway, Steve Reich, Tom Raney, *John Cage: Three Dances; Steve Reich: Four Organs; Igor Stravinsky: The Rite of Spring* (Angel Records): The details here are for the CD reissue of the 1973 Angel LP—the CD adds a four-piano arrangement of *The*

Rite of Spring, which makes this superior. It's also a look into music history, with magnificent American conductor Michael Tilson Thomas playing one of the four organs, with Reich and two other keyboardists—MTT took part in the world premiere at the Guggenheim in 1970, then in 1973 played it in Carnegie Hall. He's been entertaining audiences for decades by telling them that during that performance, "One woman walked down the aisle and repeatedly banged her head on the front of the stage, wailing 'Stop, stop, I confess.'" La plus ça change.

#

The final discographical item has less minimalism than any other, and instead has the roots of the music and it's future, which may or may not even remain in post-minimalism but move to something beyond. It's an illustration in sound of where musical ideas come from, how they pass through time and cultures, changing both and being changed by both. More than any single album, or perhaps composition, it shows how minimalism is such a powerful and natural musical tool, and that just as much as it was created by composers in the West, it may also be something that has been lying in wait in the human mind, there to be (re)discovered.

In 2003, French pianist Pierre-Laurent Aimard put out an album on Teldec titled *African Rhythms*, one of the most valuable releases in the entire minimalist discography. By this date, composer György Ligeti had finished the last of his Études. These are among the greatest works in the piano literature, the only thing holding them back from the widespread performances Glass's Etudes have had is their extreme difficulty. Ligeti takes the technical possibilities of the instrument and pushes them to the edges using a combination of velocity, polyphony, and complex syncopations and polyrhythms. It's the style that's the thing, though; Ligeti takes a mix of boogie-woogie, Debussy, African rhythms, and Reich-ian minimalism[7] and synthesizes it all into a voice that's hyper-articulate, poetic, even subversive.

Aimard was the first to record all the Études, and he plays six of them on this album, and in between there are tracks of traditional vocal and percussion music performed by the Aka Pygmies from south-western Central Africa, and Aimard also performs Reich's *Clapping Music* and *Music for Pieces of Wood*. This isn't eclecticism; Aimard shows in sound how common ideas about rhythm can be expressed in multiple, varied ways while still talking to each other. It's a mind-opening album, and a hell of a listen. Minimalism from the past, present, and into the future—outward, onward, and upward.

[7]   Many of the details themselves come through the experimental player piano music of Conlon Nancarrow.

Bibliography

Fink, Robert, *Repeating Ourselves: American Minimal Music as Cultural Practice*. University of California Press, 2005.

Gann, Kyle, *Music Downtown: Writings from the Village Voice*. University of California Press, 2006.

Glass, Philip, *Music by Philip Glass*. Harper & Row, 1987.

Glass, Philip, *Words without Music*. Liveright, 2015.

Gopinath, Sumanth, and Pwyll ap Siôn, eds., *Rethinking Reich*. Oxford University Press, 2019.

Johnson, Tom, *The Voice of New Music*. Editions 75, 1989. https://editions75.com/Books/TheVoiceOfNewMusic.PDF.

Kostelanetz, Richard, and Robert Flemming, eds., *Writings on Glass: Essays, Interviews, Criticism*. Schirmer, 1998.

Margulis, Elizabeth Hellmuth, *On Repeat: How Music Plays the Mind*. Oxford University Press, 2013.

Mertens, Wim, *American Minimal Music*. Kahn & Averill, 1988.

Nyman, Michael, *Experimental Music: Cage and Beyond*. Cambridge University Press, 1999.

O'Brien, Kerry, and William Robin, eds., *On Minimalism*. University of California Press, 2023.

Potter, Keith, *Four Musical Minimalists*. Cambridge University Press, 2002.

Potter, Keith, Kyle Gann, and Pwyll ap siôn, eds., *The Ashgate Research Companion to Minimalist and Postminimalist Music*. Routledge, 2024.

Reich, Steve, *Writings on Music*. Oxford University Press, 2002.

Reich, Steve, *Conversations*. Hanover Square Press, 2022.

Schneider, Anna, ed., *Meredith Monk Calling*. Hatje Cantz, 2024.

Schwarz, K. Robert, *Minimalists*. Phaidon, 1996.

Strickland, Edward, *Minimalism: Origins*. Indiana University Press, 2000.